Continuing recovery, but many speed bumps

- The Pacific is now expected to sustain another year of contraction in 2021 after a forecast of 1.4% growth in the Asian Development Outlook was revised down to -0.6% in the Asian Development Outlook Update. Economic prospects in Papua New Guinea (PNG) are weighed down by weak mining and petroleum output, and a worsening pandemic situation, though an improved outlook for the extractives sector should boost gross domestic product (GDP) growth next year. The regional outlook also reflects the adverse impact of continuing coronavirus disease (COVID-19) containment measures, particularly border restrictions, on business activities and tourism in the Cook Islands, Fiji, Palau, Samoa, Tonga, and Vanuatu. The subregion is forecast to rebound by 4.7% in 2022, from the previous projection of 3.8%, as wider vaccination coverage permits progressive border reopening which is expected to boost trade and tourism, particularly in the Cook Islands, Fiji, and Vanuatu. Along with PNG and Solomon Islands, the aforementioned countries account for the bulk of the growth forecast in 2022.

- The global economic recovery continues. The International Monetary Fund forecasts global growth of 5.9% in 2021, a slight decrease from its 6.0% projection in July, while the 2022 forecast remains unchanged at 4.9%. Resurgent outbreaks of COVID-19 driven by the highly transmissible Delta variant continue to weigh on economic activity and have worsened supply disruptions, exacerbating growth risks and policy trade-offs. The varying paths at which the pandemic continues to evolve across countries mean that the global recovery also remains uneven with the emergence of the Omicron variant adding further uncertainty. Near-term prospects have darkened for many developing economies partly because of limited COVID-19 vaccination. Developing Asia is now projected to grow by 7.1% this year, down from ADB's July forecast of 7.2%, and 5.4% in 2022. Growth paths continue to diverge within the region in favor of economies that have benefited from high vaccination coverage.

- The United States (US) economy recovered to its pre-pandemic level after growing by 6.3% in the first quarter and by 6.6% in the second quarter of this year. Strong consumption underpinned growth in the first half, bolstered by initially rapid progress in vaccination and sustained stimulus payments. Nevertheless, the second quarter outturn was weaker than expected and, while vaccination has eased pressure on the health system, a Delta variant-driven resurgence in COVID-19 cases clouds the outlook. The US economy is now expected to grow by 6.0% in 2021 and 4.0% in 2022. A deterioration in the pandemic path because of more infectious variants remains the key downside risk to the outlook. Gradual monetary policy tightening is expected in 2022 against a backdrop of rising inflation caused, in part, by international supply shocks.

- The economy of the People's Republic of China recovered further in the first half of 2021. Improved domestic demand and robust exports supported the first half growth of 12.7%, bouncing back strongly from a pandemic-induced slowdown in 2020. The third quarter GDP growth, however, has since slowed to 4.9% on the back of weaker investment particularly in real estate, and disruptions in the shipping and energy sectors. Growth of 8.1% is expected in 2021 and 5.5% in 2022. The unpredictability of COVID-19 outbreaks and new variants pose a downside risk to consumer demand. External risks include further supply chain disruptions, price hikes in commodities and shipping costs, and outbreaks in key trade partners weakening demand for exports.

- Renewed COVID-19 outbreaks and accompanying restrictions have also dampened consumption and slowed recovery in Japan. The economy contracted by 3.6% in the third quarter of 2021 after growth of 1.5% in the second quarter and contracting by 4.1% in the first quarter. Overall, private consumption is down year-to-date as outbreaks prompted government restrictions on business activities and mobility. This is expected to delay the

GDP Growth in Developing Asia (%, annual)

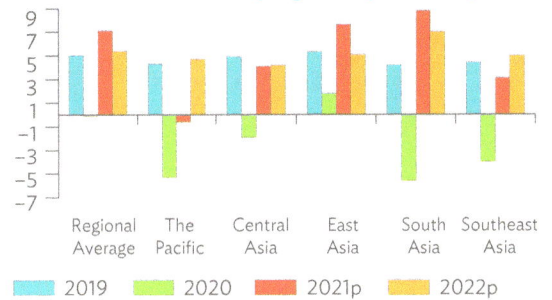

2019   2020   2021p   2022p

GDP = gross domestic product, p = projection.
Source: ADB. 2021. *Asian Development Outlook 2021 Update: Transforming Agriculture in Asia.* Manila (September).

GDP Growth (%, annual)

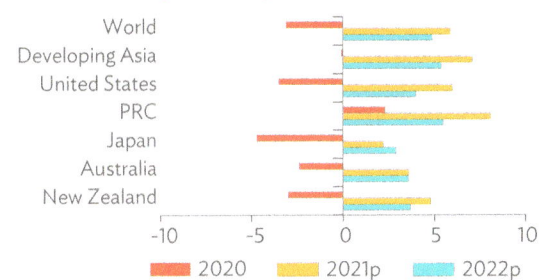

2020   2021p   2022p

GDP = gross domestic product, p = projection, PRC = People's Republic of China.
Notes: Developing Asia as defined by ADB. Figures are based on ADB estimates except for world gross domestic product growth.
Sources: ADB. 2021. *Asian Development Outlook 2021 Update: Transforming Agriculture in Asia.* Manila (September); Consensus Economics, Inc. 2021. *Asia Pacific Consensus Forecasts.* London (November); and International Monetary Fund. 2021. *World Economic Outlook: Recovery during a Pandemic–Health Concerns, Supply Disruptions, Price Pressures.* Washington, DC (October).

Vaccination Coverage in the Pacific (% of total population)

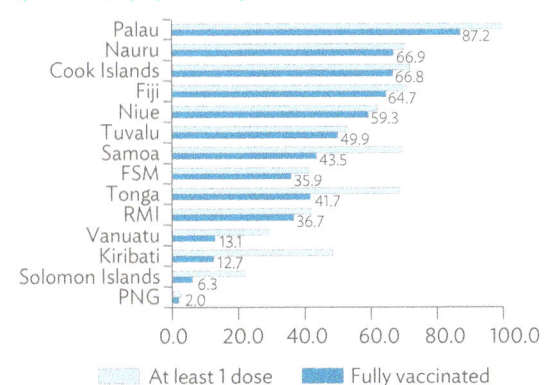

Country	Fully vaccinated
Palau	87.2
Nauru	66.9
Cook Islands	66.8
Fiji	64.7
Niue	59.3
Tuvalu	49.9
Samoa	43.5
FSM	35.9
Tonga	41.7
RMI	36.7
Vanuatu	13.1
Kiribati	12.7
Solomon Islands	6.3
PNG	2.0

At least 1 dose   Fully vaccinated

FSM = Federated States of Micronesia, RMI = Republic of the Marshall Islands, PNG = Papua New Guinea.
Note: Data as of 22 November 2021.
Sources: ADB. Asian Development Outlook Datasheet; Pacific Data Hub. COVID-19 vaccination. https://stats.pacificdata.org/vis?lc=en&df[ds]=SPC2&df[id]=DF_COVID_VACCINATION&df[ag]=SPC&df[vs]=1.0&pd=2021-02-02%2C&dq=D..&ly[cl]=INDICATOR&ly[rw]=TIME_PERIOD (all accessed 29 November 2021); and authors' calculations.

COVID-19 Cases in Pacific Developing Member Countries

	Total cases	Active cases	Total deaths	Total cases /1,000 population
PNG	35,237	576	546	3.94
Fiji	52,532	758	697	58.60
Solomon Islands	20	–	–	0.03
Palau	8	–	–	0.44
Vanuatu	6	2	1	0.02
RMI	4	–	–	0.07
Samoa	3	–	–	0.02
FSM	1	–	–	0.01
Tonga	1	–	–	0.01
World	263,246,922	20,268,106	5,237,047	33.43

FSM = Federated States of Micronesia, PNG = Papua New Guinea, RMI = Republic of the Marshall Islands.
Notes: Data as of 1 December 2021. The reported COVID-19 cases for Kiribati are not included since the patients are border cases.
Sources: ADB. Asian Development Outlook Datasheet; Worldometer. Worldometer COVID-19 Data and Population. Retrieved from: https://www.worldometers.info/coronavirus/#countries (accessed 1 December 2021); authors' calculations.

Public Debt
(% of GDP)

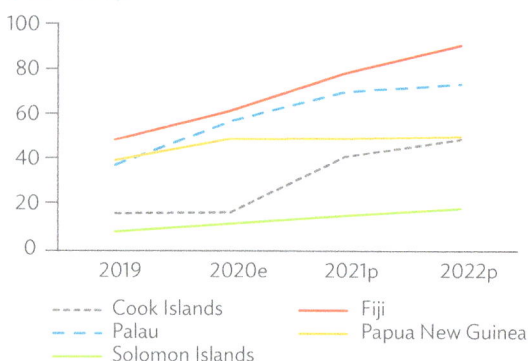

e = estimate, GDP = gross domestic product, p = projection.
Source: ADB estimates.

Average Spot Price of Brent Crude Oil
(monthly, $/barrel)

Source: World Bank. *World Bank Commodity Price Data (Pink Sheet)*. https://www.worldbank.org/en/research/commodity-markets (accessed 15 November 2021).

recovery, and GDP growth projections are revised downward to 2.2% (from 2.6%) in 2021 but upward to 2.9% (from 2.7%) in 2022. Increased vaccination coverage should support consumption moving forward, while investment and manufacturing become a growth tailwind as temporary supply constraints subside. Major downside risks are slower vaccine rollout and variant-driven outbreaks, but additional fiscal stimulus is an upside risk.

- In Australia, the economy managed to sustain growth, albeit slower, in the second quarter of 2021. Seasonally adjusted GDP rose 0.7% in the June quarter, lower than the 1.9% growth recorded in the first quarter of 2021. Domestic demand drove economic growth, led by household spending and public investment, but was offset by declines in net exports. Spending on services, particularly tourism-related activities because of the opening of trans-Tasman travel bubble with New Zealand, supported private consumption while state and local government infrastructure projects buoyed public investment. However, movement restrictions have had a detrimental impact on the economy. Growth is projected to be 3.6% in 2021 and 3.6% in 2022.

- New Zealand's economy surged in the second quarter of 2021, growing much faster than expected. The economy's seasonally adjusted GDP advanced by 2.8%, indicating a strong rebound from a recession last year, mainly because of success in controlling the virus within its borders and reopening its economy ahead of other developed economies. The second quarter growth greatly benefited from the tourism sector with the opening of a trans-Tasman travel bubble with Australia. However, the outbreak of the Delta variant in August has put the travel bubble on hold and resulted in the reinstatement of stricter restrictions in parts of the country. Despite the temporary pause, the updated full-year forecasts are 4.8% for 2021 and at 3.7% for 2022.

- Debt sustainability risks are rising as border closures and a pause in international tourism have resulted in wide government financing needs amid ongoing economic declines. With collapsing government revenues and increased spending needs to support health and countercyclical measures, public debt is seen to rise by more than 30 percentage points of GDP in the Cook Islands, Fiji, and Palau. More moderate increases in public debt ratios are projected in PNG, Samoa, Solomon Islands, Tonga, and Vanuatu. For some of the smaller Pacific economies, sustained access to grant assistance from development partners is allowing for steady declines in debt burden, but risks remain high. Country-specific debt sustainability risks will depend on the terms associated with respective portfolios, particularly concerning debt repayment schedules and possible interest rate movements.

Resurgence in commodity prices to contribute to higher inflation in the Pacific

- Crude oil prices soared in the latest quarter with the recovery of global economic activity outpacing oil production. Brent crude oil prices surged by 71% in the third quarter of 2021 (year-on-year). Adverse weather conditions in certain parts of the world have increased energy use for heating and cooling. Meanwhile, oil supply recovered slowly as a result of supply disruptions and production constraints. The full-year forecast for 2021 indicates that average crude oil prices are expected to rise 67%, reflecting upgraded global economic outlook although renewed outbreaks of the COVID-19 pandemic continue to pose an important downside risk. Agricultural commodity prices sustained their ascent in the third quarter of 2021, with the World Bank's food price index jumping 32% because of stronger-than-expected feed demand and production shortfalls earlier this year. Although the production of wheat, maize, and rice are expected to increase, strong consumption growth is expected to offset increase in supply. The food price index is expected to rise by 28% for 2021, but will stabilize in succeeding years. The downside risks to the forecast include volatile input prices and the start of the La Niña weather pattern.

- The price of liquefied natural gas jumped 75% in the third quarter of 2021 driven by a sharp increase in demand, especially in the People's Republic of China,

Food Prices
(2018 = 100, annual)

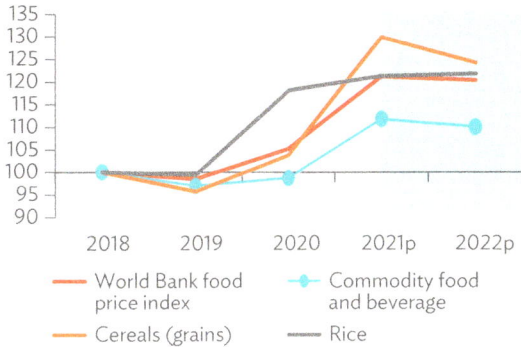

p = projection.
Source: ADB calculations using data from World Bank. 2021. *Commodity Markets Outlook: Urbanization and Commodity Demand, October 2021*. Washington, DC. and World Bank Commodity Price Data (Pink Sheet). https://www.worldbank.org/en/research/commodity-markets (accessed 15 November 2021).

Prices of Export Commodities
(2018 = 100, annual)

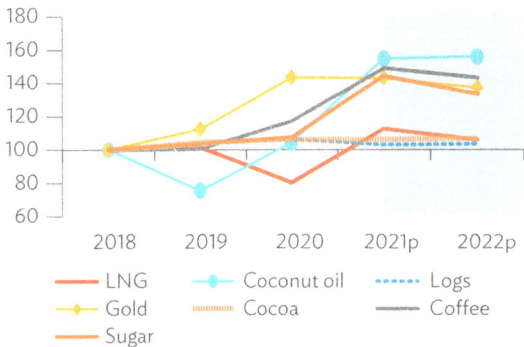

LNG = liquefied natural gas; p = projection.
Source: ADB calculations using data from World Bank. 2021. *Commodity Markets Outlook: Urbanization and Commodity Demand, October 2021*. Washington, DC and World Bank Commodity Price Data (Pink Sheet). https://www.worldbank.org/en/research/commodity-markets (accessed 15 November 2021).

Returning Residents from Pacific Destinations
('000 persons, January–August totals)

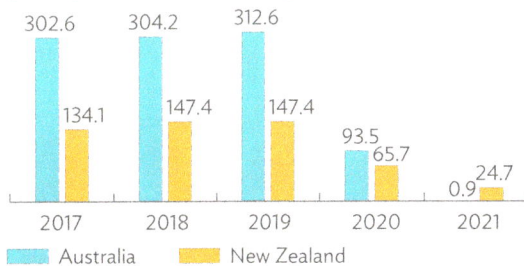

Note: Pacific destinations include the Cook Islands, Fiji, Samoa, Tonga, and Vanuatu.
Sources: Australian Bureau of Statistics and Statistics New Zealand.

Lead authors: Noel Del Castillo, Remrick Patagan, and Rommel Rabanal.

as well as limited supply disrupted mainly by adverse weather events. The full-year 2021 price forecast for liquefied natural gas is now adjusted to grow by 41% from the previous forecast of a 5% contraction. However, it is still expected to follow a downward trend in succeeding years. Gold prices fell 6% in the third quarter of 2021 amid a rise in interest rate yields and reduced gold purchases by central banks. While the full-year decline in average gold prices for 2021 is expected to be negligible, declines in succeeding years are projected to be more pronounced.

Reopening to vaccinated tourists is key to the tourism outlook

- Tourism to Pacific destinations continued to be restricted, with visitors mostly coming through travel bubble arrangements with bilateral partners. However, these arrangements had to be suspended amid risks related to the global surge in COVID-19 cases because of the Delta variant. Sustainable resumption of safe travel will be critical for near-term tourism in the Pacific. In turn, this will depend on progress in vaccination rollouts, which has so far been uneven with near universal coverage of eligible populations in the Cook Islands, Niue, and Palau versus slow uptake in Melanesian countries.

- In Palau, a travel bubble with Taipei,China commenced in April and, in more than 7 weeks, about 300 tourists arrived. The bubble was suspended at the end of May because of COVID-19 outbreaks in Taipei,China, but recommenced in August with streamlining in health protocols, along with the opportunity to receive COVID-19 vaccinations while in Palau. Since July 2021, Palau has been open to fully vaccinated travelers, but flights are so far limited to those arriving from Guam. Discussions are ongoing to expand available flight connections for fully vaccinated tourists.

- The Cook Islands likewise commenced a travel bubble with New Zealand on 17 May. More than 24,000 travelers visited the Cook Islands between May and August when the scheme was suspended on 17 August because of a COVID-19 outbreak in New Zealand. Quarantine-free travel to the Cook Islands is expected to resume in January 2022. New Zealand's trans-Tasman bubble with Australia, suspended since July, partly resumed in late-October. However, only one-way quarantine-free travel from New Zealand's South Island to destinations in Australia is allowed under this partial reopening, pending further improvements in the domestic COVID-19 situations in both countries. Fiji reopened its borders to fully vaccinated tourists in December. This reopening for the holiday season is open to a broad range of countries, including its main source markets of Australia, New Zealand, and the United States; key partners in Asia such as Japan, the Republic of Korea, and Singapore; as well as most of its Pacific peers. Health safety protocols are being supported by a Care Fiji business certification and contact tracing app to ensure that tourists' interactions are limited to similarly fully vaccinated people.

- Continuing progress in national vaccination rollouts, along with strengthening of health systems and protocols, will be critical to sustaining the nascent tourism recovery. Sustained reopening and steady recovery in visitor arrivals will then help in rebuilding the Pacific's travel and tourism sector—which has seen airlines operating at only about 8% of pre-pandemic seating capacity and overall sector unemployment rates reaching up to 80%—as a main engine of private sector-led growth in the subregion over the medium to longer term.

COUNTRY ECONOMIC ISSUES

Fiscal consolidation for economic recovery in the Cook Islands

Lead author: Lily-Anne Homasi

The Cook Islands, in common with other tourist-dependent economies in the Pacific, has been severely impacted by the coronavirus disease (COVID-19) pandemic (Figure 1). Border closures implemented to protect the population from COVID-19 eliminated tourist arrivals from 21 March 2020 to 16 May 2021 and again from 17 August 2021. This severely impacted employment and household and government incomes, and caused the economy to contract by 5.9% in fiscal year (FY) 2020 (ended 30 June) and a further 26.0% in FY2021.[1] In response to the downturn, the government mobilized a fiscal stimulus package which increased the fiscal deficit from the equivalent of 2.9% of gross domestic product (GDP) in FY2020 to 28.5% of GDP in FY2021, and the debt-to-GDP ratio from 17.1% in FY2020 to 49.1% in FY2021 (Table 1). To support medium- to long-term growth, the government embarked on a fiscal and economic recovery reform program focusing on implementing measures that would put the Cook Islands on a sustainable footing in the years ahead. This article discusses the key elements of the current fiscal and economic recovery program and draws lessons that could be useful for other Pacific developing member countries (DMCs).

Figure 1: GDP Growth of Tourism-Dependent Economies

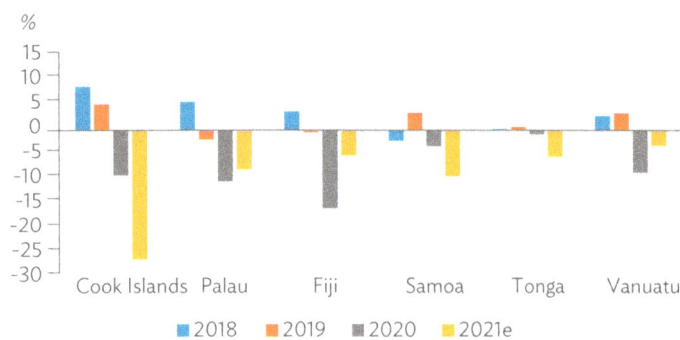

COVID-19 = coronavirus disease, e = estimate, GDP = gross domestic product.
Note: Growth estimates refer to fiscal years ending 30 June in the Cook Islands, Samoa, and Tonga; fiscal years ending 30 September in Palau; and calendar years for Fiji and Vanuatu.
Source: Asian Development Outlook database.

Prior to the pandemic, the Cook Islands had a sound macroeconomic framework with average annual GDP growth of 6.7% over FY2016–FY2019.[2] Prudent fiscal management contributed to fiscal surpluses that averaged the equivalent of 4.6% of GDP during this period, enabling accumulation of cash reserves of $91.0 million (25.8% of FY2020's GDP), with $13.0 million legislatively protected to meet debt servicing requirements. Under the previous Cook Islands fiscal framework, the fiscal deficit could not exceed 1.9% of nominal GDP unless there was an economic shock—the Cook Islands adhered to this framework in 19 of the 20 years prior to COVID-19.[3] Revenue increased from 36.4% of GDP in FY2016 to 42.3% in FY2019. Expenditure was contained, averaging 37.5% of GDP over FY2016–FY2019. Public debt was 17.1% of GDP in FY2020, down from a peak of 26.4% of GDP in FY2016.[4]

WHY IS FISCAL CONSOLIDATION IMPORTANT FOR RECOVERY?

According to the Organisation for Economic Co-operation and Development (OECD) (2001), fiscal consolidation refers to concrete fiscal policies aimed at reducing budget deficits and debt accumulation. This centers on revenue, expenditure, and debt, and the interrelationship between these factors. Evidence suggests that consolidating and backtracking nonproductive government spending, focusing expenditure on productive sectors, and mobilizing initiatives to raise revenues would help set forth a path for recovery. It is anticipated that this will be the case in the Cook Islands. Between FY2020 and FY2021, capital spending as a percentage of GDP was raised from 11.6% to 14.7% to stimulate economic activity during a slow period but is expected to decline dramatically, averaging 6.6% in FY2023–FY2024 (below pre–COVID-19 times), as tourism receipts recover to pre-pandemic levels (Table 1).[5] Debt-to-GDP ratio is expected to peak in FY2022 (reflective of additional borrowing) before receding to 35.6%, within the pre–COVID-19 range, in FY2024. Tax revenues (as a percentage of GDP), although subdued in FY2021 because of negligible tourist numbers, are expected to bounce back as tourist arrivals pick up between FY2022 and FY2024 and fiscal surplus (as a percentage of GDP) is restored by FY2024.

Table 1: Cook Islands Fiscal Framework
(% of GDP)

Item	FY2019	FY2020	FY2021e	FY2022p	FY2023p	FY2024p
Total revenue and grants	42.3	42.8	44.3	50.8	34.9	35.8
of which: tax revenue	29.0	28.1	21.7	25.2	27.7	30.6
Total expenditure	37.3	45.7	72.8	65.2	35.1	32.9
of which: wages and salaries	11.3	12.5	17.4	17.6	15.2	14.2
Capital expenditure	9.1	11.6	14.7	14.2	6.8	6.4
Overall balance (including grants)	5.0	(2.9)	(28.5)	(14.4)	(0.3)	2.9
Public debt	21.4	17.1	41.9	49.6	41.3	35.6

( ) = negative, e = estimate, FY = fiscal year, GDP = gross domestic product, p = projection.
Sources: Cook Islands Ministry of Finance and Economic Management. 2021. *Cook Islands Government Budget Estimates 2021/22*. Rarotonga; and Asian Development Bank estimates.

Elements of fiscal recovery. To pave a steady path to economic recovery, the government not only mobilized fiscal stimulus packages that moderated the extent of the contraction in the economy and livelihoods in the short term, but also devised a fiscal and economic recovery program that focuses on the Economic Recovery Roadmap (ERR), revised Medium Term Fiscal Strategy (MTFS), and a Survival and Cash Management Strategy (SCMS). These three elements supported the design of ADB's proposed policy-based loan for Supporting Sustainable Economic Recovery Program (endnote 4)[6] and lessons from this program are expected to sustain the Cook Islands in the short and medium term, in line with the government's Economic Development Strategy (EDS) 2030 to promote sustainable economic growth.[7]

- **Element 1: COVID-19 Economic Recovery Roadmap.** The road map prioritizes eight areas that will support the EDS 2030: (i) reducing the cost of borrowing (lowering interest rates for borrowers); (ii) managing the burden of public debt, in particular borrowing at the cheapest interest rates; (iii) infrastructure investment; (iv) reducing barriers to competition and business; (v) productivity growth; (vi) improved public sector efficiency; (vii) growing the labor force and preventing depopulation; and (viii) attracting foreign investment that will benefit the Cook Islands. Components such as managing the burden of public debt, productivity growth, improved public sector efficiency, and infrastructure investment directly support the MTFS. Overall, the ERR summarizes the rationale for the priority areas, actions, and the government agencies responsible for the implementation of the relevant actions. Nonetheless, the ERR could benefit from a mapping exercise to properly prioritize and sequence actions under the eight focus areas, including the identification of critical capacity gaps for implementation and opportunities for interagency cooperation. A monitoring and reporting framework similar to the detail provided for the Economic Response Program phases over 2020 and 2021 could also help to govern the implementation and monitoring of progress. The ERR could also benefit from having a risk management matrix appended to the document broadly outlining key risks and how these will be mitigated and managed. Aside from this, the ERR sets the broad parameters of the government's strategy—outlining the subset of reform actions, including the necessary revision made to the MTFS outlining its incremental and phased approach to fiscal consolidation.

- **Element 2: Revised Medium Term Fiscal Strategy.** The MTFS specifically captures fiscal rules informing the budget ceiling and boundaries on net debt, fiscal balance, expenditure, and cash reserves as well as operational rules—personnel ratio and the stabilization account. Negligible tourist arrivals in FY2020 and FY2021 (resulting in low government revenue) and large fiscal stimulus have depleted reserves and led to a liquidity crisis that forced the government to revise its fiscal rules to facilitate additional borrowing (the maximum allowable debt-to-GDP ratio was increased from 35% to 65%) and allow emergency cash management measures (the cash reserves target was reduced from 3 months expenditure cover to 1 month cover). To determine the medium-term expenditure profile, the revised MTFS also continues to use fiscal space measures: the structural ceiling approach[8] and the cyclical adjusted balance to support the fiscal space.[9] The MTFS also placed emphasis on adjusting capital spending if external financing is not secured. The revised debt-to-GDP threshold would allow the government to borrow additional funds from lenders to support reforms and infrastructure investment, if grant finance is not forthcoming to stimulate economic activities that would increase government and household incomes. Overall, the MTFS provides a clear framework to support the existing requirements and the path for recovery.

- **Element 3: Survival and Cash Management Strategy.** The SCMS directly links to elements 1 and 2, in line with the EDS. These three elements, with the support of development partners such as ADB and New Zealand, work in tandem to chart a clear path during these challenging times, and set out the scenario planning and risk assessment applied to monitoring progress against the MTFS. Each scenario reflects the level of risk and the corresponding path that will be taken by the government to manage its cash liquidity risks. There are limited options for emergency cash liquidity and, therefore, it is critical that scenarios are closely aligned with government's intentions to improve its cash position. For instance, in a best-case scenario where the suspension of the quarantine-free travel is less than 2 months, the path taken would involve the government utilizing its remaining reserves and ERR contingency budget and taking on a $40 million (12.9% of GDP in FY2021) loan to enable the government to sustain core operations and support prioritized investments. However, in a worse-case scenario where the quarantine-free travel is suspended for more than 5 months, government cash reserves would have been depleted, requiring further borrowing and extensive cuts to government spending including core operations, and limiting its ability to fully recover by FY2025, as per the revised MTFS. Scenario planning and implementation not only informs the monitoring of liquidity risks and the government's cash position, but it also facilitates dialogue to leverage additional development partner support in line with the government's recovery efforts.

Lessons for the subregion and concluding remarks. The Cook Islands' structural fiscal surplus position, low debt, and accumulated cash reserves pre–COVID-19 crisis have helped to cushion the impact of low tourist arrivals. Its commitment to transparency and openness to accepting external technical advice worked well and complemented its much smaller institutional capacity. The Cook Islands is among the few countries in the subregion with a clear fiscal and economic recovery program that is readily available online, in line with international best practice. The program contains key policy documents, including the revised MTFS, the SCMS, and other subproject documents, that acknowledge the Cook Islands' financial struggles and operational plans to overcome the challenges and ensure that the government machinery is intact. Limited capacity and technical know-how may slow implementation progress, but with the appropriate sequencing of financial and technical support, the Cook Islands experience could be replicated in and tailored to the context of relevant Pacific DMCs. Lessons will not only aid the Cook Islands' efforts to refine its approach for economic recovery, but could inform efforts of other Pacific DMCs to steer their own path to economic recovery.

Endnotes

[1] ADB. 2021. *Asian Development Outlook Update: Transforming Agriculture in Asia.* Manila.

[2] Asian Development Bank estimates.

[3] Government of the Cook Islands. 2021. *Cook Islands Government Budget Estimate 2021–2022.* Rarotonga.

[4] ADB. Forthcoming. Proposed Policy-Based Loan and Precautionary Finance Option Loan to the Cook Islands for the Supporting Sustainable Economic Recovery Program.

[5] Tourist arrivals equaled to 171,550 in FY2019, Ministry of Finance and Economic Management, Rarotonga.

[6] If approved, the program will provide much-needed financing to mitigate the liquidity crisis in the Cook Islands.

[7] Government of the Cook Islands. 2021. *Cook Islands Economic Development Strategy 2030.* Rarotonga.

[8] Estimates the difference between the structural fiscal balance and nominal fiscal balance.

[9] Accounts for the effects of business cycle fluctuations on revenue and expenditure.

References

ADB. 2021. *Asian Development Outlook Update: Transforming Agriculture in Asia.* Manila.

ADB. Forthcoming. Proposed Policy-Based Loan and Precautionary Finance Option Loan to the Cook Islands for the Supporting Sustainable Economic Recovery Program.

Government of the Cook Islands. 2021. *Cook Islands Government Budget Estimate 2021–2022.* Rarotonga.

Government of the Cook Islands. 2021. *Cook Islands Economic Development Strategy 2030.* Rarotonga.

Government of the Cook Islands. 2021. *COVID-19 Economic Recovery Roadmap.* Rarotonga.

Government of the Cook Islands, Ministry of Finance and Economic Management. 2021. *Medium Term Fiscal Framework Update.* Rarotonga.

Government of the Cook Islands, Ministry of Finance and Economic Management. 2021. *Survival and Cash Management Strategy.* Rarotonga.

OECD. 2001. *OECD Glossary of Statistical Terms - Fiscal Consolidation Definition.* https://stats.oecd.org/glossary/detail.asp?ID=984.

OECD. 2011. Fiscal Consolidation: Targets, Plans and Measures. *OECD Journal on Budgeting.* Vol. 11/2. http://dx.doi.org/10.1787/budget-11-5kg869h4w5f6.

Reducing gender inequality for a sustainable recovery in Fiji

Lead authors: Isoa Wainiqolo and Noel Del Castillo

Coronavirus disease (COVID-19) has resulted in a 2-year cumulative 20% economic contraction in Fiji. Recent estimates suggest that economic recovery may take several years to recoup lost ground, with a high degree of uncertainty. Rebuilding the economy requires unlocking potential sources of growth.

Since 2005, little has changed, with female labor participation equivalent to only half of its male counterpart. Compared to subregional peers, Fiji's gender gap, defined as the difference between male and female labor participation rate, stands at 39% in the 2015/16 survey, while the latest figures available for the Cook Islands, Kiribati, and the Federated States of Micronesia averaged 12%.[1] Although the Asian Development Bank (ADB) and other development partners have increased focus on narrowing this gap in Fiji over the years, reform opportunities remain to support the post–COVID-19 pandemic recovery.

FIJI ECONOMIC RECOVERY

Fiji was one of the hardest-hit economies in the Pacific subregion when the COVID-19 pandemic pushed governments worldwide to implement border closures and movement restrictions. From 2010 to 2018, tourism and travel-related services were the main drivers of economic growth, contributing an average of 34% to gross domestic product (GDP) and 26% to total employment (Wainiqolo 2021). With the onset of the pandemic and the global travel restrictions, the collapse of the tourism sector resulted in the deepest economic contraction ever recorded for Fiji, with GDP falling by 15.7% in 2020. A further contraction of 5.0% is projected for 2021.

A second wave of COVID-19 community transmission brought about by the highly contagious Delta variant resulted in a jump in the number of confirmed cases (active plus recovered) from only 72 in mid-April 2021 to more than 52,000 at the end of October. This necessitated the government's continued support for the unemployed and those in the informal sector.[2]

The government is banking heavily on its efforts to vaccinate the eligible population to achieve economic recovery. As of 22 November 2021, 97.1% of Fiji's eligible population had received a first dose of the COVID-19 vaccine while 90.2% were fully vaccinated. This has allowed authorities to resume domestic interisland travel and reopen international borders to Fiji passport and working visa holders from 11 November 2021, and selected travel partners from 1 December 2021.[3]

The response to Fiji's reopening plans has been positive with significant forward bookings received by hotels and Fiji Airways. It has been reported that some travel agents are finding it difficult to find spaces in selected resorts in the period between Christmas and New Year[4] while a notable travel agent selling joint hotels and airfare packages has recorded historical daily takings from Australians.[5]

Jetstar, an Australian budget airline, has also recorded a 200% increase in bookings compared to pre–COVID-19 levels for travel to Fiji.[6] While the collaborative effort by tourism stakeholders in Fiji is commendable, the risk of new COVID-19 variants remains. Any wrong move would be costly, considering investments made to reopen.

As it prepares the economy for eventual reopening, the government needs to ensure that its finances are properly managed to accelerate economic recovery. There are several policy actions that the government can take, as discussed in the country article for Fiji in the July 2021 issue of the *Pacific Economic Monitor* (Wainiqolo 2021). In its September 2021 Article IV Mission, the International Monetary Fund (2021) suggested continued government support to the economy in the short term, but efforts must be taken to address the broader macroeconomic imbalance once recovery takes hold. Fiscal consolidation strategies should focus on growth-friendly revenue measures and restrained expenditure levels, which are crucial to put debt on a downward trajectory.

Aside from sound fiscal management, there are other areas that the government can pursue to chart a sustainable recovery post-pandemic. The *Asian Development Outlook 2021* highlighted the challenge of unlocking the potential in Fiji's primary sector as an economic alternative to improve its resilience to shocks. Another area worth looking at is increasing women's participation in the labor force, which can contribute to higher productivity and sustainable recovery, and improve other development outcomes.

GENDER INEQUALITY

Pre-pandemic, Fiji's male labor force participation rates increased or were relatively stable in all survey periods, in line with the country's GDP per capita trend (Figure 2). On average, female labor participation has only been half of the male equivalent. Much of women's economic activity is informal and unrecognized, such as small-scale or backyard farming while unpaid domestic work is usually completed by women. About 7 in every 10 women outside the labor force were involved in housework compared to less than 1 in 20 men, while 1 in 2 men outside the labor force were involved in full-time studies compared to 1 in 5 women. Although there was an increase in female labor participation between 2005 and 2012, the gender gap remained relatively unchanged since then, with female participation averaging 42% and male participation at 80%.

On a global scale, Fiji was ranked 113th out of 156 countries in a recent gender gap index report (World Economic Forum 2021). As shown in Figure 3, Fiji performed well on educational attainment and health and survival index compared to the "ideal" benchmark (close to zero, indicating lesser disparity), but poorly on political empowerment as well as on economic participation and opportunity (closer to 1, indicating greater disparity). Fiji was ranked higher overall than neighboring countries Papua New Guinea (135th) and Vanuatu (141st), but around similar levels as comparably-sized countries, such as Maldives (128th) and Mauritius (110th).

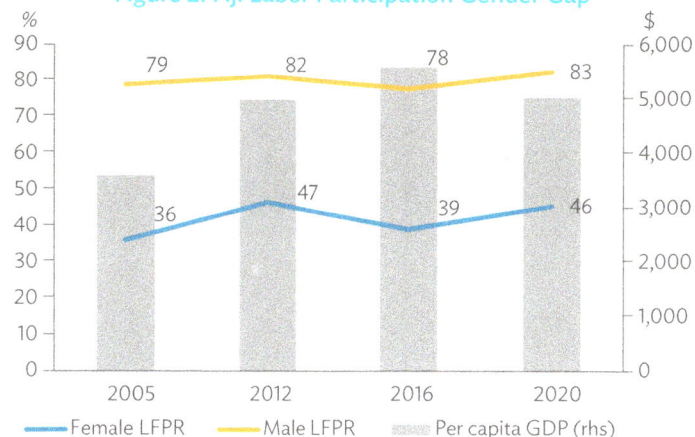

Figure 2: Fiji Labor Participation Gender Gap

GDP = gross domestic product; LFPR = labor force participation rate; rhs = right-hand scale.
Sources: Asian Development Bank estimates; and Fiji Bureau of Statistics. Employment Statistics. https://www.statsfiji.gov.fj/statistics/social-statistics/employment-statistics44.html (accessed 24 November 2021).

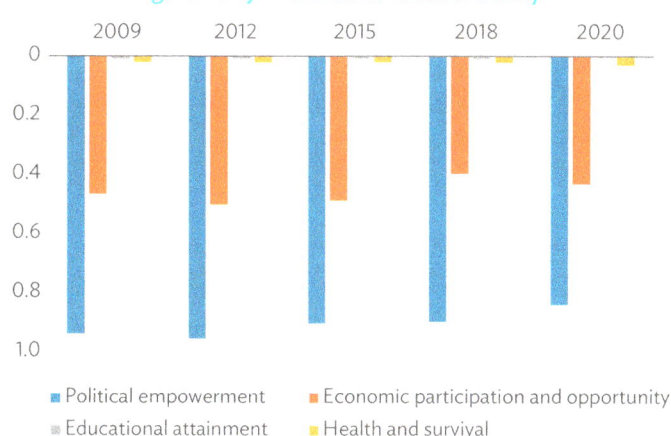

Figure 3: Fiji Distance to Gender Parity

Note: Closer to 1 indicates greater disparity.
Source: Asian Development Bank estimates using data from World Economic Forum. *Global Gender Gap Reports* (various years). Geneva.

In the 2020 Human Development Report, Fiji was ranked 84th out of 162 countries in gender inequality, which measures inequalities between women and men in reproductive health, empowerment, and economic activity. Fiji's score was better than the average for least-developed countries and small island developing states, but worse than that for East Asia and the Pacific.

An ADB technical assistance report (ADB 2016) investigated reasons behind low female labor force participation in selected Asian economies and in the literature. It highlighted major constraints to female labor force participation, including domestic responsibilities, discrimination, limited information, and high cost of accessing work for women. The report offered policy suggestions, such as having quotas, increased information provision, and legal reforms to encourage women's participation.

RECENT RESEARCH ON THE GROWTH CONTRIBUTION OF GENDER EQUITY

An IMF study on the economic gains from gender equality identified two channels through which gender can contribute to economic growth (Ostry et al. 2018). First, women bring into the workplace new skill sets and perspectives. The paper found that male and female labor are complementary in production, which increased overall productivity.

Second, women play a vital role in the growth of the services sector. Women in Fiji are more likely to have better labor participation rates in the wholesale and retail trade industry; manufacturing; accommodation and food services; human health and social work; and professional, scientific, and technical activities. However, most of these sectors were severely affected by COVID-19. As the economy recovers, the demand for the services sector is expected to gradually improve and, consequently, the demand for more female workers.

Removing gender disparities leads to higher per capita income. A paper by Kim, Lee, and Shin (2016) found that eliminating gender disparities between men and women in the Republic of Korea could raise female labor force participation from 54.4% to 67.5% and per capita income growth from 3.6% to 4.1% over a generation. In a simulation, the paper finds that the policies that eliminate discrimination in the labor market were the most effective in raising per capita incomes.

DEVELOPMENT PARTNER EFFORTS TO NARROW THE GENDER GAP IN FIJI

The focus on gender in Fiji is not something recent. It has been an area of interest/support for decades for key stakeholders, such as the United Nations, the Government of Australia, the Government of New Zealand, regional bodies such as the Pacific Islands Forum Secretariat, The Pacific Community, the World Bank, and the International Finance Corporation (IFC), in collaboration with the Government of Fiji and nongovernment organizations.

ADB's Strategy 2030 development framework includes strengthening women's economic empowerment, enhancing gender equality, and boosting women's resilience to external shocks among its operational priorities. ADB has committed to ensuring that 75% of its committed operations promote gender equality and support climate change mitigation and adaptation by 2030.

At the project level in Fiji, ADB collaborated with other development partners to pilot gender-responsive budgeting as part of its policy-based loan in 2020.[7] In support of women's economic empowerment and building community resilience, an ADB technical assistance project partnered with Habitat for Humanity Fiji to provide women with carpentry skills that they can use to contribute and make decisions around shelter preparedness in their communities, as well as to access employment opportunities within a historically male-dominated construction industry.[8]

Based on the economic potential of addressing gender disparity, the IFC, in collaboration with the Government of Fiji, is designing Fiji's first Early Childhood Care Services Policy Framework. This is in response to an earlier study that showed that 41% of the private sector and 46% of public sector workforce had preschool-aged children (IFC 2019) but only 8% used childcare services.[9] Although both parents' work was affected, women's participation tends to be disproportionately affected because of childcare duties. Productivity of parents at work was also affected, although the difference between gender was minor. The report found that, each year, businesses and public sector in Fiji are losing about 13 workdays per employee because of the responsibilities of working parents.

POLICY RECOMMENDATIONS

Fiji set itself an ambitious target in 2019, aiming to raise annual productivity growth to 3.2% in its National Productivity 15-Year Master Plan 2021–2036—a significant increase from the 1.2% average between 1995 and 2016 (Asian Productivity Organization 2019). Minimizing the gender gap in economic participation and opportunity, and political empowerment can provide an avenue to boost economic growth beyond the services sector and improve long-term growth prospects.

To increase women's formal economic participation, the government may need to go beyond promoting their increased involvement in the workforce to setting hard targets. The government (i) incorporated significant elements of the Convention on the Elimination of All Forms of Discrimination Against Women in 1995, (ii) introduced its second Women's Plan of Action (2010–2019) and launched its national gender policy in 2014, and (iii) incorporated elements of gender equality in its 5-year and 20-year national development plans. Despite these efforts, there is no significant improvement on the gender gap that exists in the labor market (Figure 2). Household-specific concerns as well as societal norms continue to pose structural barriers that prevent more women from actively participating in formal economic activities. Meanwhile, microbusinesses, of which about 40% are owned by women and are the main source of employment for women (IFC 2021), have been heavily affected by the pandemic and would need government support for their recovery, such as accessing credit markets and providing training on running micro, small, and medium-sized enterprises. Longer-term recovery plans should include incentives (such as trainings and concessional loans for start-ups) to stimulate women's participation in potential growth areas (such as information and communication technology and green growth jobs) and seed funding to women micro, small, and medium-sized enterprises and businesses (COVID-19 Response Gender Working Group 2020).

The government may also consider increased appreciation of the care economy, with women comprising 63% of health workers in Fiji (COVID-19 Response Gender Working Group 2020). This entails the strengthening of support provided for health workers, particularly for women who usually need to juggle household care work and frontline care duties. On average, IFC survey results found that most parents were paying F$60 per week for childcare and were willing to pay F$4 more. While there is a huge potential for childcare services (with almost half for both public and private sectors workers having pre-school aged children), only 8% of parents with pre-school age children uses formal childcare services. The government can consider investing in more childcare facilities that will encourage more parents to use them. This can free up parents, particularly mothers, and allow them to focus better on their work and for other mothers to join the labor force. Passing laws that will promote and strengthen childcare protection can increase parents' confidence in the childcare services. At the same time, the growth of childcare services can provide more opportunities for more women in the formal sector employment.

With many Fijian women belonging to the informal sector of the economy, increased government support to informal workers would help in improving the gender imbalance and empower women. When the second outbreak struck in April 2021, the government extended financial support to those who lost their jobs and those belonging to the informal sector in an amount that equaled F$360 per individual for a 3-month period (endnote 2). Given its unconditional nature, a potential concern revolves around how the financial support has been used by the recipients. The program can be improved by providing incentives that encourage more productive use of the financial support, such as buying farming kits for backyard gardening, starting small-scale poultry farms, both of which can help family food security. The government can also consider extending such targeted support to vulnerable groups beyond the end of the pandemic.

Unavailability of timely and gender-disaggregated data may also be a hindrance. Establishing a core minimum set of economic indicators to track, such as (i) involvement of women in business and income generation, and (ii) types of activities and income levels of women in different economic sectors (ADB 2016) can provide key data to support policy deliberations.

CONCLUSION

The economic gains wiped out by the COVID-19 pandemic will take several years to recover. In the long run, building a more diversified economy should remain a priority. Reducing the gender gap provides an avenue for a broader and sustainable recovery that supports economic livelihoods. The biggest gain may no longer come from right-sizing the workforce but more from right-mixing gender participation.

Endnotes

[1] The Pacific Community. Pacific Data Hub. https://stats.pacificdata.org/ (accessed 17 November 2021). According to the Fiji Bureau of Statistics and International Labour Organization (2018), labor force participation rate refers to proportion of working-age population that are either working (paid or unpaid) or looking for work. It measures the size of labor supply that is available for production relative to working-age population.

[2] The government has continued supporting those unemployed because of the pandemic by topping up their withdrawable pension funds if they have exhausted a certain portion of their superannuation savings. Affected employees draw down part of their superannuation funds (general balance) first. The government will only top up those who do not have sufficient general account balance. By construction, 30% of superannuation contributions are in a general account with possible withdrawals for life-cycle events, while the rest is kept in a preserved account specifically for retirement purposes. For those above 18 years of age and were in the informal sector prior to the pandemic, payments were to be made in two batches of F$360 each, with COVID-19 vaccination as part of the criteria. A total of F$106 million was paid out in the first round of assistance in August, while the second round of payment was made in November.

[3] Fiji will operate a "traffic light system" when the borders open in December, depending on vaccination rates in source countries. Fiji will reopen first to countries which include its major tourist source markets such as Australia, New Zealand, the United States, the United Kingdom, and most Pacific island countries. Fiji will no longer use traditional quarantine requirements for these countries, but will introduce a new set of protocols such as the no-jab, no-fly policy. Other requirements include testing negative for COVID-19 within 72 hours before departure and spending the first 2 days on hotel premises. A rapid diagnostic test will be taken after 48 hours before visitors are allowed to safe-travel areas. Restrictions will remain for areas with low vaccination coverage. For fully vaccinated visitors from countries outside travel-safe list, they need to undergo a 10-day quarantine upon arrival and need to test negative for the virus before being allowed to enter the community.

[4] R. Nasiko. 2021. Operator receives 5000 bookings. *The Fiji Times*. 27 October. https://www.fijitimes.com/operator-receives-5000-bookings/.

[5] N. Wolfe. 2021. Thousands of Australians book holidays as Fiji prepares for December 1 opening. *news.com.au*. 20 October. https://www.news.com.au/travel/destinations/pacific/thousands-of-australians-book-holidays-as-fiji-prepares-for-december-1-opening/news-story/da5688f67920c0f8b7a0b1868ec275c6.

[6] G. Waldron. 2021. Qantas to bring forward A380 re-launch; eyes earlier 787-9 deliveries. *FlightGlobal*. 22 October. https://www.flightglobal.com/fleets/qantas-to-bring-forward-a380-re-launch-eyes-earlier-787-9-deliveries/146041.article.

[7] ADB. 2020. *Report and Recommendation of the President to the Board of Directors: Proposed Policy-Based Loan for Subprogram 3 Republic of Fiji: Sustained Private Sector-Led Growth Reform Program*. Manila.

[8] ADB. 2021. *Green Jobs for Women: Construction Skills for Fijian Women*. Video. Manila. 19 August. https://www.adb.org/news/videos/green-jobs-women-construction-skills-fijian-women.

[9] A. Vakasukawaqa. 2021. Gender program commended. *The Fiji Times*. 13 October. https://www.fijitimes.com/gender-program-commended/.

References

Asian Development Bank (ADB). 2016. *Fiji Country Gender Assessment 2015*. Manila.

ADB. 2016. *Female Labor Force Participation in Asia - Constraints and Challenges*. Consultant's report. Manila (Project Number 47363-001).

Asian Productivity Organization. 2019. *Fiji National Productivity Master Plan 2021-2036*. Tokyo.

COVID-19 Response Gender Working Group. 2020. *Gendered Impacts of COVID-19 on Women in Fiji*. http://www.fwrm.org.fj/images/Gender_and_COVID_Guidance_Note_-_Rapid_Gender_Analysis.pdf.

Fiji Bureau of Statistics. 2018. *2017 Population and Housing Census*. Suva.

Fiji Bureau of Statistics and International Labour Organization. 2018. *Fiji Employment and Unemployment Survey 2015-2016*. Suva.

International Finance Corporation. 2019. *Tackling Childcare: The Business Case for Employer-Supported Childcare in Fiji*. Washington, DC.

International Labour Organization and United Nations Development Programme. 2018. *Time-use surveys and statistics in Asia and the Pacific*. Geneva.

International Monetary Fund. 2021. Republic of Fiji 2021 Article IV Consultation. *IMF Country Report*. No. 21/257. Washington, DC.

Kim, J., J.-W. Lee, & K. Shin. 2016. Impact of Gender Inequality on the Republic of Korea's Long-term Economic Growth: An Application of the Theoretical Model of Gender Inequality and Economic Growth. *ADB Economics Working Paper Series*. No. 473. Manila: ADB.

Ostry, J. D., J. Alvarez, R. Espinoza, & C. Papageorgiou. 2018. Economic Gains from Gender Inclusion: New Mechanisms, New Evidence. *IMF Staff Discussion Note*. No. 18/106. Washington, DC: IMF.

The Pacific Community. Pacific Data Hub. https://stats.pacificdata.org/ (accessed 17 November 2021).

Wainiqolo, I. 2021. Treading a fine line: assessing Fiji's economic recovery efforts amid a new pandemic wave. *Pacific Economic Monitor*. Manila: ADB (July).

World Economic Forum 2021. 2021. *Global Gender Gap Report 2021*. https://www.weforum.org/reports/global-gender-gap-report-2021.

Future-proofing fisheries in the Federated States of Micronesia

Lead author: Remrick Patagan

Border closures and movement restrictions in response to the coronavirus disease (COVID-19) have forced many societies to revisit the importance of subsistence agriculture and fisheries. In the Federated States of Micronesia (FSM), as in other Pacific developing member countries (DMCs), the fisheries sector is particularly important for food and economic security (Figure 4). Royalties from offshore fishing have become a major source of government revenues.

Beyond the current challenges from COVID-19, however, the world is facing an equally serious and long simmering crisis through climate change. Commitments made at the recent 26th United Nations Climate Change Conference of the Parties (COP26) still fall far short of what is needed to meet the United Nations' climate goals of net zero carbon emissions by 2050 and limiting global warming within 1.5°C–2.0°C.

Figure 4: Federated States of Micronesia Offshore Fisheries

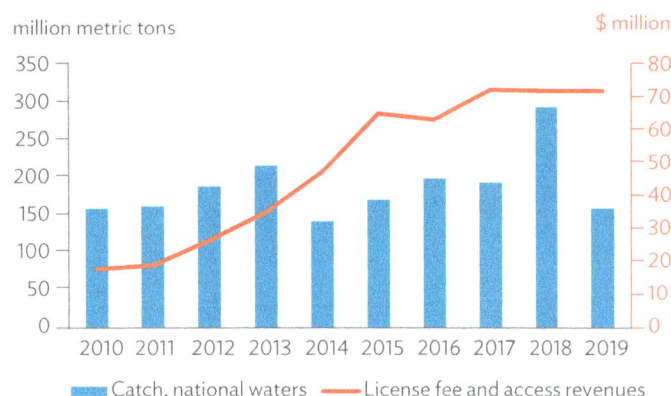

Source: Pacific Forum Fisheries Agency. 2021. *Economic and Development Indicators and Statistics: Tuna Fisheries of the Western and Central Pacific Ocean 2020.* https://www.ffa.int/node/2596 (accessed 3 November 2021).

Yet, even with an optimistic outcome, the effects of climate change that we are experiencing today and are likely to see in the future are, in the words of a British broadsheet, already "inevitable, unprecedented, and irreversible."[1] The Intergovernmental Panel on Climate Change (IPCC)[2] reports that practically all existing coral reefs will decline under the target warming level of 2°C. At the "ideal" level of 1.5°C, the world will still see a 70%–90% decline in live coral cover. This has implications for food security through cascade effects on fisheries ecosystems (Figure 5), and the economy through loss of incomes and government revenues.

Similarly, a synthesis report[3] on the impacts of climate change on fisheries and agriculture by the Food and Agriculture Organization of the United Nations (FAO) has the following takeaways:

- Global warming is likely to affect food webs that are supporting key tuna species, and very likely to cause changes in distribution and abundance of tuna by 2050 under a business-as-usual emissions scenario.
- Redistribution of tuna is very likely to affect license fee revenues from purse-seine fishing and shift more fishing into international waters (Figure 6). Harvest strategies will need to account for changes in distribution and abundance that result from climate change.
- Global warming, extreme events, and ocean acidification are very likely to damage coral reefs and other habitats underpinning small-scale, coastal fisheries for demersal fish and invertebrates. Changes to coral reefs and other fish habitats, and the direct effects of carbon dioxide emissions on fish and invertebrates, are likely to reduce harvests from small-scale, coastal fisheries

by up to 20% by 2050, and by up to 50% by 2100, under a high emissions scenario.

- Climate change is likely to increase uncertainty in replenishment of coastal fish stocks, requiring a more conservative community-based ecosystem approach to fisheries management. Priority adaptations to maintain the benefits of coastal fisheries involve minimizing the gap between sustainable harvests and the fish needed for food security, and filling the gap mainly by increasing access to tuna for small-scale fishers.

Effects on coastal fish habitats. Under a business-as-usual emissions scenario, coral reefs in all Pacific DMCs will experience severe annual bleaching by 2050. Along with ocean acidification, the resulting decline in live coral cover means that most existing reefs will give way to macroalgae by 2100, affecting the overall productivity and species composition of coastal habitats.

Effects on distribution and abundance. For offshore fisheries, climate change will alter the abundance and distribution of tuna. Under a business-as-usual emissions scenario, the distribution of skipjack and yellowfin will shift eastward with decreases in abundance in the FSM, Nauru, Palau, and Papua New Guinea. Bigeye populations are projected to decline across the exclusive economic zones of all Pacific DMCs, while albacore are expected to shift south towards the Tasman Sea. For coastal fisheries, the direct and indirect effects of climate change could reduce productivity of bottom-dwelling fish in the Western and Central Pacific by 50% or more by 2100 (Bell et al. 2011). Such changes could threaten the viability and sustainability of commercial fisheries by 2050.

Implications for food and economic security. Lower catches of skipjack and yellowfin and redistribution of bigeye and albacore would affect license revenues in Pacific DMCs. In terms of food security, climate change will worsen an already precarious situation and, in the FSM,[4] small-scale coastal fisheries underpinning food and livelihoods remain especially vulnerable. This is because much of the catch is derived from coral reefs.

Consequences for fisheries management. In the case of offshore fisheries, climate change is expected to bring about changes in abundance and distribution of fish and specifically tuna species. The FSM is likely to be vulnerable to these changes. It will benefit from regional cooperation through the Western and Central Pacific Fisheries Commission and the Inter-American Tropical Tuna Commission. Along with other small countries that depend on license fees, the FSM is expected to be vulnerable to these changes by 2050.

For coastal fisheries, climate change will increase uncertainty in the replenishment of coastal stocks and increase the gap between demand and sustainable supply. While sustainable production levels in the FSM are expected to continue to meet demand until 2030, any potential gap can be filled by diversifying target species through near-shore fisheries for tuna and other pelagic species for small-scale fishers. On coastal fisheries management, there is need for informing stakeholders about risks and involving them

in decision-making; better interdisciplinary monitoring of impacts and identification of practical adaptations; and strong climate-informed, community- and ecosystem-based approaches to fisheries management.

A lot of knowledge gaps remain to be filled to enhance fisheries management and properly assess the impacts of climate change, both at the global level and on economies such as the FSM. Collection of better data and improved simulations are particularly important.

While the FSM benefits from regional fisheries management institutions that produce valuable knowledge including stock assessments and simulations on productivity and distribution of fish catches, the data environment for coastal fisheries leaves much to be desired. Poor data on coastal fisheries production create considerable difficulty in accurately portraying fishery benefits and managing climate-related threats accordingly.

Subsistence fishing in the FSM is thought to be grossly underreported.[5] Based on consumption data, alternative numbers on coastal fishery production by the Secretariat of the Pacific Community in 2015[6] show higher production estimates than those by FAO. Of domestic production in 2014, subsistence fishing accounted for about 73% with the rest from commercial fishing. By type of fishery products, reef fish make up 70% with the rest accounted for by ocean fish (24%) and invertebrates (6%). Dependence on subsistence- and reef-based fisheries makes the FSM's island communities highly vulnerable to climate change.

Reliable data are crucial not only for coastal ecosystems and fisheries management, but also for assessing localized impacts of climate change. Development of localized data could support the case for more drastic international action on mitigation and mobilizing more funding for adaptation in the most vulnerable countries. Recent work by the World Bank with the Marshall Islands[7] and by ADB with Tonga[8] are examples of such initiatives, though these have focused on physical assets. The FSM could pursue similar studies that could focus on localized impacts of climate change on ecological assets like coral reefs.

It is becoming increasingly apparent that the negative effects of climate change can no longer be avoided. Consequently, adaptation and mitigation efforts by the FSM and the rest of the world become ever more necessary in order to avert even worse climate impacts.

One possible solution that could address both mitigation and adaptation needs, as well as being a blue economy opportunity, is marine permaculture.[9] The concept hinges on artificial upwelling, a geoengineering intervention that uses deep water pumps to stimulate the flow of nutrient-rich cold water at the bottom of the ocean to the surface. The technology is not new, but marine permaculture utilizes it to irrigate seaweed farms that could serve as an alternative food source, habitat for marine life, and carbon sink at sufficient scale.[10]

In addition, situating marine permaculture installations near coral reefs could help protect them from rising surface temperatures. It is also well-suited to future oceanic conditions that favor the growth of seaweeds and are characterized by losses in fisheries productivity. Work on marine permaculture initially focused on subtropical environments and kelp farming, but there is scope for the FSM and other Pacific DMCs to learn from the use of the technology in tropical contexts in American Samoa and the Philippines.

Under increasingly difficult prospects for emissions reductions, geoengineering measures have attracted attention though they are argued as a complement, rather than an alternative, to climate mitigation. These interventions have their own disadvantages, and their viability is as yet unproven at scale. But in an increasingly warming world, countries need to consider all possible solutions. The most vulnerable ones like small island developing states can no longer ignore the imperative of climate adaptation at home even as they clamor for ambitious mitigation abroad. Future-proofing the FSM's fisheries will determine whether the country sinks or swims with the tide of climate change.

Figure 5: Projected Changes, Impacts, and Risks for Ocean Ecosystems as a Result of Climate Change

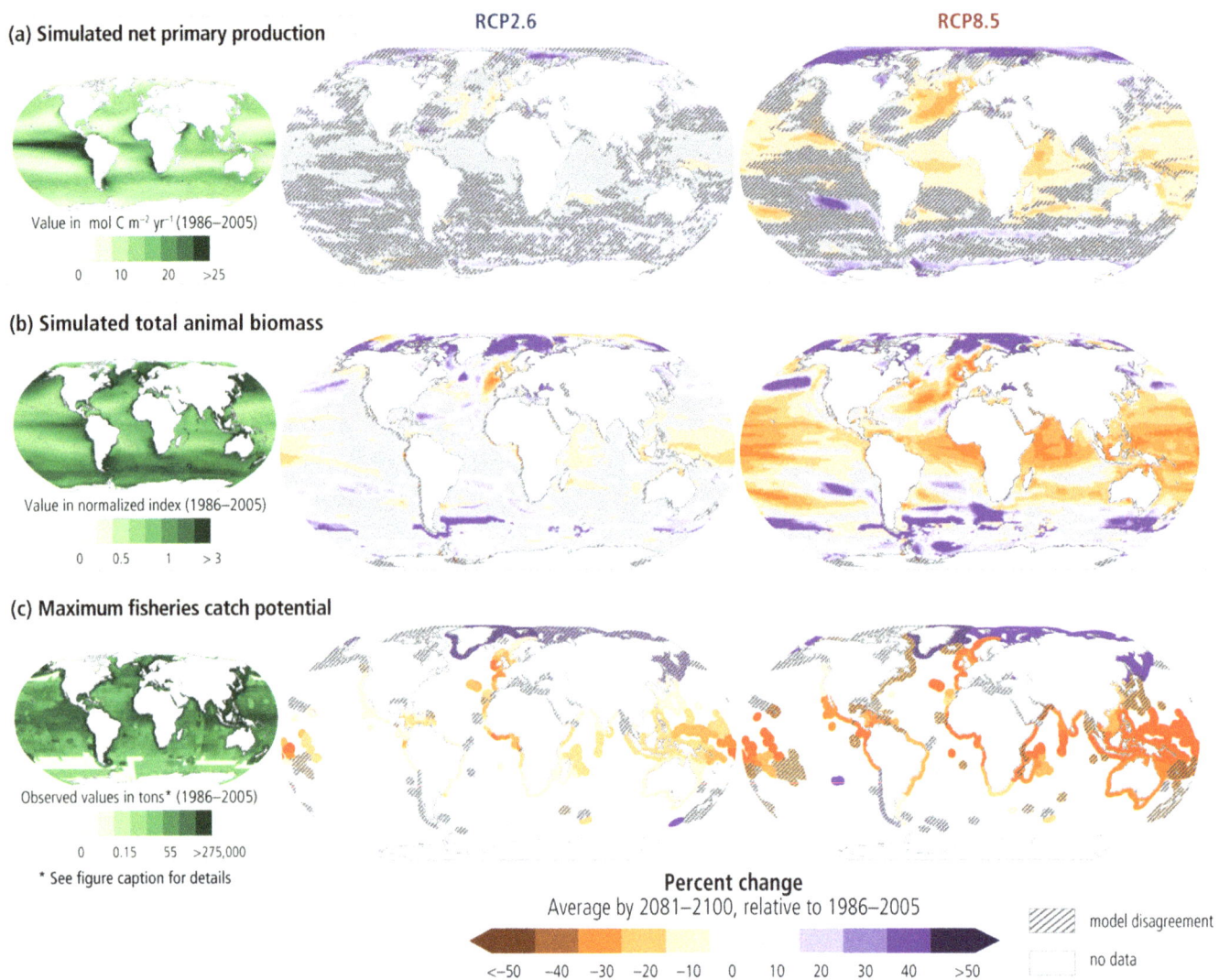

RCP = representative concentration pathway, mol C -²yr-² = mass of carbon per unit area per year.
Source: Intergovernmental Panel on Climate Change (IPCC). 2019. *Summary for Policymakers.* https://www.ipcc.ch/srocc/download/. Figure SPM.3 (ABC) in IPCC Special Report on the Ocean and Cryosphere in a Changing Climate. H.-O. Pörtner, D.C. Roberts, V. Masson-Delmotte, P. Zhai, M. Tignor, E. Poloczanska, K. Mintenbeck, A. Alegría, M. Nicolai, A. Okem, J. Petzold, B. Rama, and N.M. Weyer (eds). In press. p. 23.

Figure 6: Projected Changes in Tuna Distributions as a Result of Climate Change

Average historical (2005) distributions of skipjack, yellowfin and bigeye tuna and South Pacific albacore (Mt/km^2) in the tropical Pacific Ocean, and projected changes in biomass of each species relative to 2005 under the RCP8.5 emission scenario for 2050 and 2100, simulated using SEAPODYM. Isopleths in the projections for 2050 and 2100 represent the relative percentage change in biomass caused by climate change

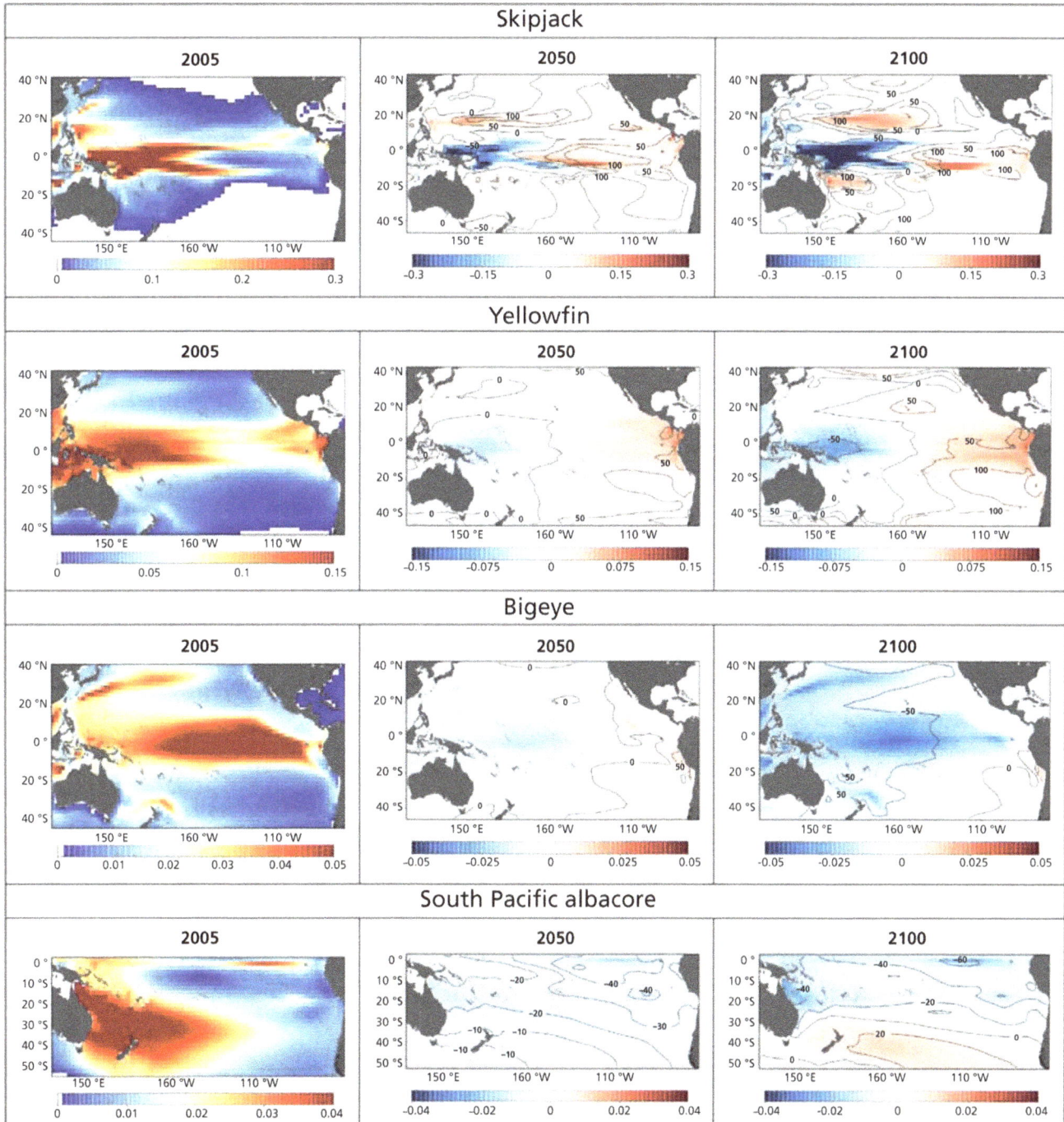

RCP = representative concentration pathway, Mt/km^2 = metric tons per square kilometer, SEAPODYM = Spatial Ecosystem and Population Dynamics Model.
Source: Food and Agriculture Organization of the United Nations. 2018. *Impacts of climate change on fisheries and aquaculture: Synthesis of current knowledge, adaptation and mitigation options.* http://www.fao.org/3/I9705EN/i9705en.pdf. Reproduced with permission.

Endnotes

[1] *The Guardian.* 2021. 'Code red for humanity': what the papers say about the IPCC report on the climate crisis. 10 August.

[2] IPCC. 2019. *IPCC Special Report on the Ocean and Cryosphere in a Changing Climate.* H.-O. Pörtner, D.C. Roberts, V. Masson-Delmotte, P. Zhai, M. Tignor, E. Poloczanska, K. Mintenbeck, A. Alegría, M. Nicolai, A. Okem, J. Petzold, B. Rama, and N.M. Weyer (eds). https://www.ipcc.ch/srocc/download/.

[3] FAO. 2018. *Impacts of climate change on fisheries and aquaculture: Synthesis of current knowledge, adaptation and mitigation options.* http://www.fao.org/3/I9705EN/i9705en.pdf.

[4] J. D. Bell, J. Johnson, A. Hobday (eds). 2011. *Vulnerability of Tropical Pacific Fisheries and Aquaculture to Climate Change.* Secretariat of the Pacific Community. https://coastfish.spc.int/component/content/article/412-vulnerability-of-tropical-pacifc-fisheries-and-aquaculture-to-climate-change.html.

[5] Vali et al. 2014. *Working Paper #2014-06: Reconstruction of total fisheries catches for the Federated States of Micronesia (1950–2010).* Vancouver: Fisheries Centre, University of British Columbia. http://www.seaaroundus.org/doc/publications/wp/2014/Vali-et-al-Federated-States-of-Micronesia.pdf.

[6] R. D. Gillet. 2016. *Fisheries in the Economies of Pacific Island Countries and Territories.* Pacific Community.

[7] World Bank. 2021. Marshall Islands: New Climate Study Visualizes Confronting Risk of Projected Sea Level Rise. Press release. https://www.worldbank.org/en/news/press-release/2021/10/29/marshall-islands-new-climate-study-visualizes-confronting-risk-of-projected-sea-level-rise.

[8] ADB. 2021. *ADB,* Tonga Launch Joint Disaster Risk Management Work at COP26. Press release. https://www.adb.org/news/adb-tonga-launch-joint-disaster-risk-management-work-cop26.

[9] Climate Foundation. *Marine Permaculture.* https://www.climatefoundation.org/marine-permaculture.html.

[10] Climate Foundation. 2019. *Marine Permaculture Offshore Executive Summary.* https://www.climatefoundation.org/uploads/3/0/2/0/30209783/marine_permaculture_exec_summ_august_2019_two_pager.pdf.

References

ADB. 2021. ADB, Tonga Launch Joint Disaster Risk Management Work at COP26. Press release. https://www.adb.org/news/adb-tonga-launch-joint-disaster-risk-management-work-cop26.

Asch, R. G., W. W. L. Cheung, and G. Reygondeau. 2018. Future marine ecosystem drivers, biodiversity, and fisheries maximum catch potential in Pacific Island countries and territories under climate change. *Marine Policy.* 88: 285–294. https://doi.org/10.1016/j.

marpol.2017.08.015. Cited in FAO. 2018. *Impacts of climate change on fisheries and aquaculture: Synthesis of current knowledge, adaptation and mitigation options.* http://www.fao.org/3/I9705EN/i9705en.pdf.

Bell, J. D., J. Johnson, and A. Hobday (eds). 2011. *Vulnerability of Tropical Pacific Fisheries and Aquaculture to Climate Change.* Secretariat of the Pacific Community. https://coastfish.spc.int/component/content/article/412-vulnerability-of-tropical-pacifc-fisheries-and-aquaculture-to-climate-change.html.

Bell, J. D., M. Kronen, A. Vunisea, W. J. Nash, G. Keeble, A. Demmke, S. Pontifex, and S. Andrefouet. 2009. Planning the use of fish for food security in the Pacific. *Marine Policy*, Volume 33, Issue 1, pp. 64–76. https://www.sciencedirect.com/science/article/abs/pii/S0308597X08000778.

Climate Foundation. *Marine Permaculture.* https://www.climatefoundation.org/marine-permaculture.html.

Climate Foundation. 2019. *Marine Permaculture Offshore Executive Summary.* https://www.climatefoundation.org/uploads/3/0/2/0/30209783/marine_permaculture_exec_summ_august_2019_two_pager.pdf.

FAO. 2018. *Impacts of climate change on fisheries and aquaculture: Synthesis of current knowledge, adaptation and mitigation options.* http://www.fao.org/3/I9705EN/i9705en.pdf.

Gillet, R. D. 2016. *Fisheries in the Economies of Pacific Island Countries and Territories.* Pacific Community.

IPCC. 2019. *IPCC Special Report on the Ocean and Cryosphere in a Changing Climate.* H.-O. Pörtner, D.C. Roberts, V. Masson-Delmotte, P. Zhai, M. Tignor, E. Poloczanska, K. Mintenbeck, A. Alegría, M. Nicolai, A. Okem, J. Petzold, B. Rama, and N.M. Weyer (eds). https://www.ipcc.ch/srocc/download/.

Pacific Forum Fisheries Agency. 2021. *Economic and Development Indicators and Statistics: Tuna Fisheries of the Western and Central Pacific Ocean 2020.* https://www.ffa.int/node/2596. (accessed 3 November 2021).

The Guardian. 2021. 'Code red for humanity': what the papers say about the IPCC report on the climate crisis. 10 August.

Vali, S., K. Rhodes, A. Au, K. Zylich, S. Harper, and D. Zeller. 2014. *Working Paper #2014-06: Reconstruction of total fisheries catches for the Federated States of Micronesia (1950–2010).* Vancouver: Fisheries Centre, University of British Columbia. http://www.seaaroundus.org/doc/publications/wp/2014/Vali-et-al-Federated-States-of-Micronesia.pdf.

World Bank. 2021. Marshall Islands: New Climate Study Visualizes Confronting Risk of Projected Sea Level Rise. Press release. https://www.worldbank.org/en/news/press-release/2021/10/29/marshall-islands-new-climate-study-visualizes-confronting-risk-of-projected-sea-level-rise.

Exploring a recovery path for labor mobility in Kiribati and Tuvalu

Lead authors: Noel Del Castillo, Lily-Anne Homasi, and Isoa Wainiqolo

The coronavirus disease (COVID-19) pandemic has affected all aspects of life in Kiribati and Tuvalu, although less severely compared with its tourist-dependent neighbors (Figure 7). While the number of cases in these countries has been relatively low compared to subregional peers, border closures and restrictions in the movement of goods and peoples have significantly affected the livelihood of their peoples. One area that has not yet been explored is the impact of the pandemic on labor mobility. With most of the employment in both countries driven by the public sector, employment outside government is through domestic microenterprises, or through seeking employment abroad.

Figure 7: Gross Domestic Product Growth of Selected Pacific Island Countries

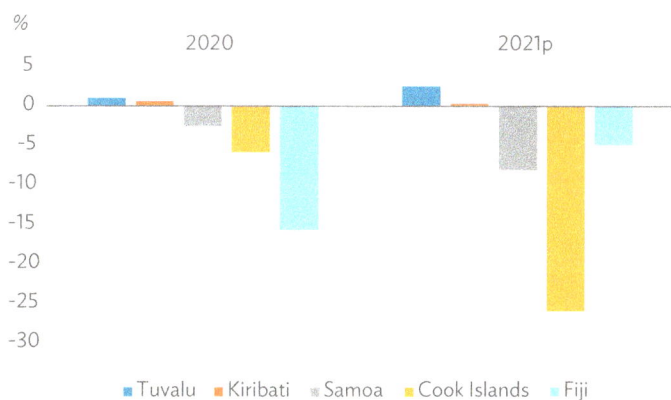

p = projection.
Note: For the Cook Islands and Samoa, the years are fiscal years ending on 30 June.
Sources: ADB. 2021. *Asian Development Outlook 2021 Update: Transforming Agriculture in Asia*. Manila; ADB estimates; and Samoa Bureau of Statistics. National Accounts. https://www.sbs.gov.ws/economics (accessed 17 November 2021).

Many I-Kiribati and Tuvaluan overseas workers find employment in Australia under the Seasonal Worker Programme (SWP) and Pacific Labour Scheme, in New Zealand under the Recognised Seasonal Employer (RSE) scheme, or as maritime workers. The pandemic has affected labor mobility in the small island economies of Kiribati and Tuvalu as well as their overseas workers who are stranded because of travel restrictions. Post-pandemic, sustaining economic growth requires policy options that can help restart the lives and livelihoods of these workers affected by the pandemic.

KIRIBATI

Kiribati is one of the few countries that has managed to keep the threat of the virus at bay and weather the economic fallout associated with the global pandemic. Unlike neighboring Pacific countries that

have tourism-dependent economies, Kiribati's economy managed to grow in 2020 and is expected to post faster growth in 2022. Given its inherently weak health system, and high prevalence of communicable and noncommunicable diseases, the Government of Kiribati understandably put in place strict border closures, which have become the country's primary protection against the virus but a cause of great distress for its overseas workers.

The labor market is dominated by the public sector, employing more than 5,000 civil servants (excluding employees in 18 state-owned enterprises). The pandemic has adversely affected many I-Kiribati workers outside of the public sector. The Government of Kiribati estimates that 50,000 men and women are eligible for unemployment benefits. In September 2020, the government introduced a new unemployment benefit to cover those affected by the pandemic. With the government intending to include this permanently as part of its social protection measures, it is estimated to cost A$30 million annually, about 10.8% of gross domestic product in 2020. During the pandemic, more than 1,000 overseas workers were impacted by the border closure with 69% unable to leave the country for deployment and 31% left stranded abroad.

One of the immediate impacts of the pandemic on overseas workers was on their earnings. A World Bank (2020) report observed that the income effects of COVID-19 have differed considerably across Pacific island countries. Among the nationalities surveyed, Samoan and I-Kiribati workers in Australia and New Zealand had the highest number of reported reductions in their earnings at 86% and 77%, respectively. I-Kiribati workers also experienced, on average, a 55% drop in their weekly earnings which is second only to Timorese workers (Figure 8). The large reductions in earnings translated to lower savings and contraction in their living expenses. Unsurprisingly, about 75% of I-Kiribati workers reported sending lower remittances, with those under the SWP reporting an average drop of 55% and those part of the RSE scheme indicating a reduction of 41%. This contrasts with the experience of Tongan workers who, in the same survey, relayed that only 38% of them have sent lower remittances—an average drop of 48% for those under the SWP and 53% for those part of the RSE scheme.

Another issue that concerns overseas I-Kiribati workers is repatriation. This is especially important for I-Kiribati seafarers who were among the maritime workers displaced when global travel restrictions disrupted the crew change system. Seafarers travel by plane to and from the ports where the ships that they will work on are docked, and COVID-19-related restrictions are hampering this process. The limited availability of commercial flights is reducing travel options for seafarers, increasing the costs of air travel to ship operators, and preventing crew changes and the repatriation of disembarking seafarers (International Maritime Organization). Border closures, tighter restrictions in visa issuance, and quarantine requirements are further complicating the situation. This has resulted in seafarers being stranded on ships with their contracts being extended repeatedly to the point that it poses potential serious consequences to their health (International Maritime Organization). Other seafarers get stranded in foreign lands where they are supposed to board repatriation flights, but the restrictions have prevented air travel as well. Such is the case for I-Kiribati seafarers who are stranded in Australia, Fiji, Germany, Indonesia, the Republic of Korea, and Spain, with some having been away for as long as 18 months, primarily because of the border closure still being implemented in Kiribati. With border restrictions extended until 31 December 2021, repatriation for I-Kiribati seafarers is becoming more difficult.

Figure 8: Percentage Reduction in Weekly Earnings of Seasonal Workers in Australia and New Zealand

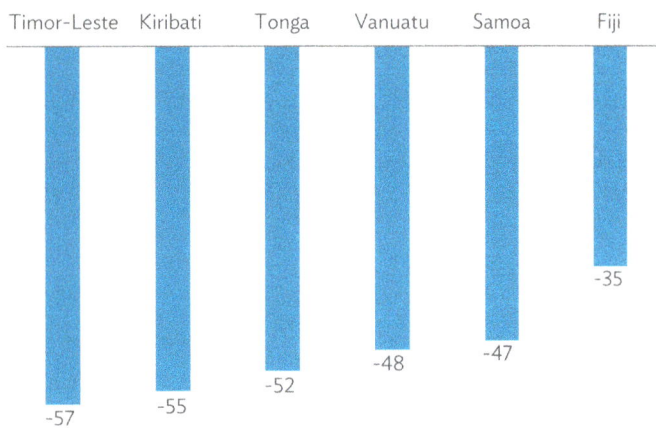

Source: World Bank. 2020. *Pacific Labor Mobility, Migration and Remittances in times of COVID-19: Interim Report.* https://documents1.worldbank.org/curated/en/430961606712129708/pdf/Pacific-Labor-Mobility-Migration-and-Remittances-in-Times-of-COVID-19-Interim-Report.pdf.

When the Government of New Zealand closed its international ports of entry on 19 March 2020, there were I-Kiribati workers who were part of the RSE. While repatriation efforts have allowed 6,551 Pacific RSE workers to return to their respective home countries, 286 I-Kiribati workers remain in New Zealand. Given the limited capacity of isolation and quarantine facilities in Kiribati, the government has deemed the repatriation of RSE workers a low priority (Bedford and Bedford 2021). Further, the absence of direct flights from New Zealand to Kiribati makes transportation costly and the April–July 2021 outbreak in Fiji, where chartered flights to Kiribati have departed, raised the risk, uncertainty, and costs for both workers and their employers. If people become wary of migrating or travel overseas for employment, this will have long-term effects on the well-being of the country and its people.

Repatriation is a central theme to any immediate policy that the government will undertake to respond to the plight of its overseas workers. This requires revisiting its isolation and quarantine procedures as well as mobilization of resources to provide the necessary facilities to accommodate repatriating I-Kiribati workers. It is also vital for the government to revisit its arrangement with the consortium of shipping companies to plan a comprehensive repatriation strategy for its citizens and ensure that it does not risk the livelihoods of its citizens that are already dependent on international seafaring.

TUVALU

Tuvalu is one of the few remaining countries in the world with zero cases of COVID-19. The swift response of its government to close ports of entry and impose movement restrictions was hinged on a weak health system that would be overwhelmed if the pandemic were to reach its shores. Aside from the high population densities, which makes it vulnerable for an outbreak, the prevalence of illnesses such as diabetes and heart disease pose comorbidity risks.

The immediate impact of the pandemic on the Tuvaluan economy has been relatively moderate compared to the tourism-dependent Pacific economies. Still, when the Government of Tuvalu declared a State of Emergency (SOE) as its response to the pandemic, the closure of ports of entry and movement restrictions had adverse impacts on Tuvaluan workers, with some reporting reductions either in total working hours or wages, and others losing their jobs altogether.

Employment in Tuvalu may be classified into two major categories: the subsistence sector, which is outside the monetary system, and the formal sector. The subsistence sector plays an important part in the country's economy by contributing to food security and alternative forms of livelihood because most Tuvaluans participate in some form of subsistence production which includes fishing, fruit and vegetable gardening, copra production, growing of livestock, house building, and various traditional food preservation activities.

On the other hand, formal sector employment is dominated by the public sector, employing more than 1,500 paid workers in the country while the total employment in the private sector is estimated at 695 workers (International Organization for Migration [IOM] and International Labour Organization [ILO] 2021). With the government being the main driver of the country's economy, employment in the civil service and state-owned enterprises is desirable mainly because of job security and attractive employment terms and remuneration packages. On the other hand, it is challenging to estimate private sector employment, given the significant number of self-employed persons running small businesses such as those in retail, restaurants, guest houses, mechanical repairs, construction, and transport. Some self-employed may not even be members of the Tuvalu National Provident Fund.

The preventive measures imposed by the government affected workers differently. In a survey conducted by IOM and ILO (2021), about 88% of the respondents indicated that the SOE declaration had somehow affected them, with notable impacts being difficulty in accessing protective equipment, reduction in the number of working hours, reduction in wages, and difficulty in securing loans.

Some businesses in Tuvalu were forced to scale down or completely shut down operations resulting in furlough of about 115 workers. Most of the affected workers came from the fisheries sectors, with about 52% of them former fisheries observers. About 67% of the laid-off workers who participated in the survey indicated that they were earning A$800 per week and 62% of them had at least six dependent family members. It was difficult for those who were laid off to find alternative jobs. One-third of those who found jobs were working in areas that did not match their skills, with most of them taking on construction- and security-related jobs. Majority of these workers were earning only half of what they used to get from previous employment (IOM and ILO 2021).

Offshore employment is another important component of the formal sector. Most of the overseas Tuvaluan workers are working in the maritime industry. Meanwhile, there are 113 Tuvaluan workers in New Zealand under the RSE program and 32 Tuvaluans in Australia under the Pacific Labour Scheme (IOM and ILO 2021).

Like Kiribati, Tuvalu was one of the three remaining Pacific countries[1] that had no repatriations of its RSE workers in New Zealand as of September 2021 (Bedford and Bedford 2021).[2] Aside from there being no direct flights between New Zealand and Tuvalu, the Government of Tuvalu is confronted with a dilemma regarding the repatriation of its overseas workers. While the government understands its duty to repatriate overseas Tuvaluans, it also recognizes that repatriation would significantly increase the risk of COVID-19 entering the country (Simeti and Marinaccio 2021). In the absence of adequate medical facilities and sufficient equipment, immediate repatriation could expose and endanger the health and well-being of domestic Tuvaluans. The dilemma on the government's repatriation program is rooted in the issue of accountability—it is responsible for the welfare of both overseas and domestic Tuvaluans.

Although Tuvalu was able to endure the immediate impacts of the pandemic better compared to its other subregional neighbors, the persistence of this global health crisis could highlight further vulnerabilities of the country. To a certain extent, the adverse impacts of the SOE declaration on domestic workers were minimized because of the government's provision of financial assistance to every Tuvaluan during the SOE. This program is not sustainable in the long run, especially with the government relying heavily on budget support and other forms of assistance from development partners. If this pandemic persists, Tuvalu needs to be fiscally prepared in case it experiences a decline in external funding support, which is estimated at 51% of gross domestic product in its recent national budget. The government should consider policies that will support the post-pandemic economic recovery of Tuvalu, such as enhancing domestic revenues and improving the efficiency of public spending.

Another concern is the issue of food security. With Tuvalu a heavy importer of food products, one of the initial concerns raised, when movement restrictions were first imposed across the world last year, was that a prolonged pandemic would not bode well for the country. In this respect, the government's policy to provide seedlings for use in home gardens, support and fast-track existing agriculture projects, and encourage landowners to practice customary stockpiling techniques (such as drying fish and root crops, preserving breadfruit, and storing coconuts) are steps in the right direction. Increased production and consumption of domestic food items can reduce dependence on imported goods and, hopefully, can improve the overall health condition of the people as they obtain more nutrition from fresh, locally sourced food (Farbotko and Kitara 2020). With

the recent resurgence in global agricultural commodity prices (page 4), the potential risk of higher inflation because of higher imported food prices can be better managed.

THE PATH FORWARD

For Kiribati and Tuvalu, labor mobility schemes play a critical role in supporting men and women to gain employment. Most of the workers under these schemes are employed in unskilled and/or semiskilled jobs in Australia and New Zealand with limited scope of securing employment in their own countries.

As borders eventually reopen post-pandemic, overseas workers will play an important role both in their home and host countries. Home countries will greatly benefit from remittance inflows and transfer of new knowledge and technical know-how to support private sector engagement, while host countries will rely on migrant laborers to address the need for vocational-skilled workers that could not be met by local supply. For example, a study shows that there is a shortage for vocational-skilled workers in Australia that could not be addressed by local labor supply and another study showing how Pacific island countries can address the labor shortage gap (Chand, Clemens, and Dempster 2021).

To capitalize on such opportunities and support a conducive environment for the labor mobility market to flourish domestically and overseas, it is critical for labor policies to reflect this intent and protect the interest of overseas workers, and build a multiskilled workforce through formal academic scholarship programs or technical and vocational education and training programs. These programs could promote entrepreneurial skills and financial literacy and could be offered at the technical institutes in these countries and through the Australian Pacific Technical Coalition.

Endnotes

[1] The other country is Nauru (Bedford and Bedford 2021).

[2] Efforts to initiate repatriation of Tuvaluan workers are expected to commence at the end of 2021.

References

Bedford, C. and R. Bedford. 2021. *RSE Repatriation: Kiribati Needs to Step Up.* https://devpolicy.org/rse-repatriation-kiribati-needs-to-step-up-20210903/.

Chand, S., M. Clemens, and H. Dempster. 2021. *Australia Needs More Pacific Mid-Skill Migration: Here's How to Facilitate it.* https://devpolicy.org/australia-needs-more-pacific-mid-skill-migration-20211015/?utm_source=rss&utm_medium=rss&utm_campaign=australia-needs-more-pacific-mid-skill-migration-20211015.

Farbotko, C. and T. Kitara. 2020. *How is Tuvalu Securing Against COVID-19?* https://devpolicy.org/how-is-tuvalu-securing-against-covid-19-20200406/.

Human Rights At Sea. 2021. I-Kiribati Seafaring Community Pleads with Government to Repatriate Stranded Colleagues. News release. 30 August. https://www.humanrightsatsea.org/2021/08/30/i-kiribati-seafaring-community-pleads-with-government-to-repatriate-stranded-colleagues/.

International Maritime Organization. Undated. *Frequently Asked Questions About How COVID-19 is Impacting Seafarers.* https://www.imo.org/en/MediaCentre/HotTopics/Pages/FAQ-on-crew-changes-and-repatriation-of-seafarers.aspx.

International Organization for Migration and International Labour Organization. 2021. *Powering Past the Pandemic: Bolstering Tuvalu's Socioeconomic Resilience in a COVID-19 World.* Suva.

Simeti, T. and J. Marinaccio. 2020. *'How is Tuvalu Securing Against COVID-19?': A Response From Funafuti.* https://devpolicy.org/how-is-tuvalu-securing-against-covid-19-a-response-from-funafuti-20200422-3/.

World Bank. 2020. *Pacific Labor Mobility, Migration and Remittances in times of COVID-19: Interim Report.* https://documents1.worldbank.org/curated/en/430961606712129708/pdf/Pacific-Labor-Mobility-Migration-and-Remittances-in-Times-of-COVID-19-Interim-Report.pdf.

Building freestanding pillars: state-owned enterprise reforms in the Marshall Islands and Palau

Lead authors: Rommel Rabanal and Cara Tinio

Prolonged border closures have successfully prevented any community transmission of coronavirus disease (COVID-19) in the North Pacific, but also resulted in severe economic and fiscal impacts. Steady progress in national vaccinations provides optimism for economic recovery commencing in FY2022 (ends 30 September 2022), but longer-term fiscal sustainability requires further adjustments. The need for such adjustments becomes more pressing given the possibility that financial assistance from the United States (US) may end when the Marshall Islands and Palau's respective Compacts of Free Association with the US expire in 2023. A key component of these adjustments is reforming state-owned enterprises (SOEs), which have needed significant fiscal transfers to sustain operations. More efficient SOEs that reduce the burden on government budgets while delivering quality services will be critical to rebalancing fiscal accounts in the Marshall Islands and Palau.

MARSHALL ISLANDS

State-owned enterprises have a broad reach and carry considerable weight in the Marshall Islands' economy. Beyond telecommunications, transport, and utilities, where SOEs commonly operate, the Marshall Islands also has SOEs active in hotel administration and copra production.

The country's 11 active SOEs hold combined assets equivalent to about 80% of gross domestic product (GDP), and those backed by government guarantees account for a third of outstanding public debt.

Although some of these enterprises have realized small operating profits, these do not offset the large losses incurred by others. This overall negative outcome is attributed to the mandate of many of these SOEs to provide public services to outer island residents alongside their commercial objectives, which makes cost recovery difficult, and lack of management capacity. Tobolar, the SOE processing copra mostly from outer island communities, is notably used to provide a safety net to farmers by paying above-market prices for copra.

Between FY2012 and FY2019, SOEs in the Marshall Islands generated a combined operating loss averaging $9.4 million (equivalent to 7.1% of GDP) every year (Figure 9). This grew by 91.8% a year in the last 3 years. Subsidies to cover these losses averaged $11.3 million (8.5% of GDP) in FY2012–FY2019, exceeding annual capital spending all through the period. Subsidies peaked at $15.5 million (11.6% of GDP) in FY2017 and declined only slightly in FY2018 and FY2019, averaging $14.3 million (10.7% of GDP) in these last 2 years.

Figure 9: Marshall Islands: Subsidies and Results of State-Owned Enterprises Operations

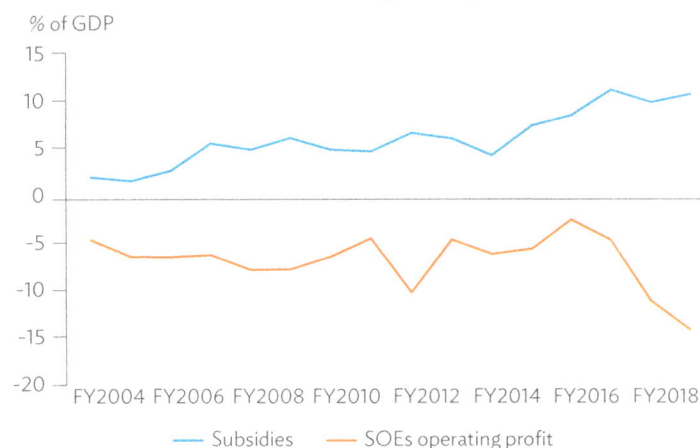

FY = fiscal year, GDP = gross domestic product, SOE = state-owned enterprise.
Note: Fiscal year ends 30 September of that year.
Source: ADB estimates based on Graduate School USA. 2021. *Fiscal Year 2020 Statistical Appendices (Preliminary).* https://pitiviti.org/storage/dm/2021/06/rmi-econstat-tabs-fy20-prelim-pub1-20210625021527687.pdf.

Since FY2004, most subsidies have gone to less than half of the Marshall Islands' active SOEs (Figure 10). The share of Tobolar increased to stand at more than 50% of total subsidies in FY2019–FY2020. Besides copra costs, general and administrative expenses have risen in recent years to almost half of sales as of FY2019. Other SOEs receiving significant subsidies are Kwajalein Atoll Joint Utility Resources, which provides power, sewerage, and water services in Ebeye (the Marshall Islands' second-largest population center); the Marshall Islands Shipping Corporation, which operates and maintains government vessels; Air Marshall Islands, the national flag carrier; and the National Telecommunications Authority, the country's sole telecommunications services provider.

Figure 10: Marshall Islands: Subsidies to State-Owned Enterprises

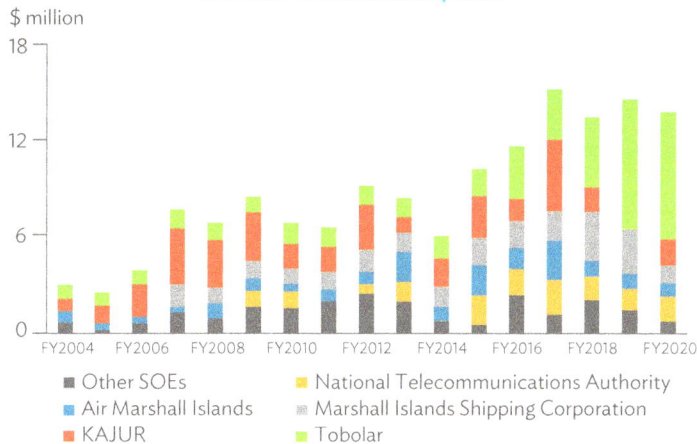

FY = fiscal year, KAJUR = Kwajalein Atoll Joint Utility Resources,
SOE = state-owned enterprise.
Note: Fiscal year ends 30 September of that year.
Source: ADB estimates based on Graduate School USA. 2021. *Fiscal Year 2020 Statistical Appendices (Preliminary)*. https://pitiviti.org/storage/dm/2021/06/rmi-econstat-tabs-fy20-prelim-pub1-20210625021527687.pdf.

Recognizing that subsidies to SOEs are a growing burden that divert government resources from critical social services and pose a significant risk to fiscal self-sufficiency, the Government of the Marshall Islands is working to improve these SOEs' efficiency and financial viability. In 2015, the Parliament passed the State-Owned Enterprises Act seeking to (i) improve SOEs' corporate governance and commercial orientation; (ii) establish guidelines for community service obligation agreements (CSOs), which specify goods and services to be provided and help inform the amount of subsidy to be received; and (iii) encourage SOEs to report regularly on their business plans and financial performance. To boost its capacity to implement this law, the Ministry of Finance (MOF) set up an SOE monitoring unit and is also receiving assistance from its reform coordination unit established with ADB support.

These enhancements have helped, but progress has been limited because of SOEs' capacity constraints and difficulties in fulfilling their commercial mandate. MOF also requires continued capacity augmentation, the provision of which has been disrupted by travel restrictions in response to the COVID-19 pandemic. Efforts to professionalize SOE boards of directors have been hampered by a 2016 amendment to the SOE Act that allows more public officials to hold directorships, and the limited availability of women qualified to serve on SOE boards, although ongoing ADB-supported training is seeking to remedy the latter. The initial set of CSOs covering four key SOEs has yet to be finalized. Reporting has improved, with nine SOEs submitting annual business plans to MOF as of 2019, but annual reports are delayed largely because of late audits to financial statements.

However, reducing subsidies must be balanced with the sustainable delivery of CSOs, given that SOEs provide essential basic services. Detailed accounting and record-keeping, by staff with the necessary skills, will help improve the estimation of the costs to deliver CSOs. More accurate information will rationalize subsidies without sacrificing service provision. There is also the need to examine the

Tobolar copra subsidy, with a view towards instituting a formal social protection system. Besides improving the efficiency of Tobolar's operations and aiding fiscal consolidation, this would better direct funds to lower-income households, especially in the outer island communities.

PALAU

The Palau Public Utilities Corporation (PPUC) was established upon the country's independence in 1994 as the state-owned utility responsible for power generation, transmission, and distribution. In 2013, through the enactment of the Utilities Consolidated Act, PPUC was reorganized as an umbrella utility that covers electricity as well as water and wastewater operations.

PPUC's electricity operations are hampered by high costs of electricity production stemming from the network's historical dependence on diesel, which contributes to 95% of generation compared with only 5% from relatively recently introduced renewables. Technical and operational issues, with grid losses at almost 16% and billed electricity at less than 70% of production, further add to inefficiencies. Electricity tariffs are regulated by the Palau Energy Administration based on cost-recovery principles. Nonetheless, residential electricity tariffs—at $0.26 per kilowatt-hour as of 2018–2019—are currently set below the cost of electricity supply, as reflected in tariffs applied to commercial, industrial, and government customers of $0.31 per kilowatt-hour. Residential electricity is also implicitly cross-subsidized through deferral of operation and maintenance spending, particularly for diesel power plants.

For water supply, Palau mostly relies on surface water sources. These include the Ngerikil and Ngerimel streams that supply the Koror–Airai water supply system, the largest system operated by PPUC. Smaller water supply systems in more remote outlying states are in disrepair absent capital investment and limited maintenance spending since 2010, resulting in limited access in these areas. Of the water produced, an estimated 48% (as of 2018) is lost to deteriorating infrastructure, illegal connections, and inaccurate metering (i.e., nonrevenue water). PPUC's water and wastewater operations are covered by legal and regulatory frameworks, established prior to the merger, that mandate operating under commercial principles and targeting full cost recovery, subject to compliance with drinking water quality standards. However, as existing water treatment facilities have been unable to meet these standards, particularly in areas outside of Koror and Airai. PPUC has been unable to raise water tariffs, which are already among the lowest in the Pacific (Figure 11). In turn, insufficient revenues have precluded any major investments to improve water supply services, resulting in an ongoing cycle of financial constraints that leads to poor service quality and vice-versa.

Weak performance of water and wastewater operations has further translated into a substantial buildup of accounts payable to the electric power operations division within PPUC, resulting in a de facto subsidization across services. Overall, PPUC has required subsidies from the national government averaging $1.5 million (or about 2.3% of the government's recurrent expenses) in 5 of the 7 years from FY2013 to FY2019, largely because of tariffs being set below full cost recovery. Although PPUC almost achieved its target of full cost recovery across electricity and water and wastewater operations, with total operating revenue reaching more than 90% of total operating expenses, legislation was passed in 2017 that froze tariffs at 2011 levels, reversing recent hard-won financial sustainability gains. Although this legislation expired in June 2018, its financial ramifications linger for PPUC.

Figure 11: Pacific Water Tariffs, Residential Average, 2020

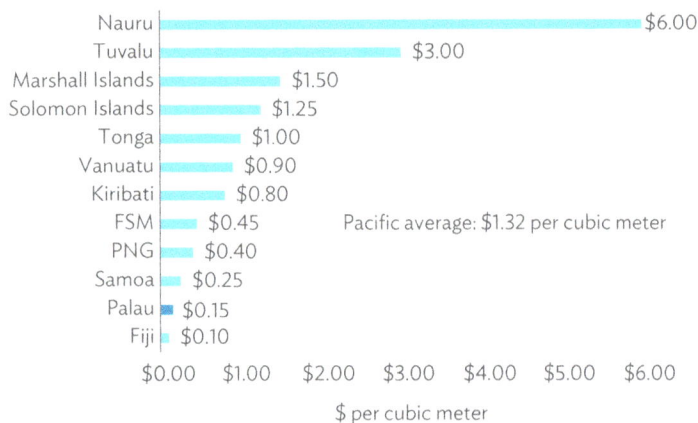

Nauru	$6.00
Tuvalu	$3.00
Marshall Islands	$1.50
Solomon Islands	$1.25
Tonga	$1.00
Vanuatu	$0.90
Kiribati	$0.80
FSM	$0.45
PNG	$0.40
Samoa	$0.25
Palau	$0.15
Fiji	$0.10

Pacific average: $1.32 per cubic meter

$ per cubic meter

FSM = Federated States of Micronesia, PNG = Papua New Guinea.
Source: Pacific Regional Infrastructure Facility. 2021. *Pacific Infrastructure Performance Indicators 2021*. Sydney (September).

The government and PPUC are embarking on a comprehensive reform program to move the utility's operations toward a more stable and sustainable financial footing. PPUC is implementing reforms to its tariffs, financial management, and corporate governance with the aim of reducing subsidy requirements. The government is also seeking to encourage more public–private partnerships (PPPs) in utility services to stimulate private sector development in public service delivery.

Several key reforms to electricity operations were completed in 2020. Among others, PPUC has developed (i) a revenue required model for electricity operations; (ii) a revenue enhancement action plan for priority investment projects, (iii) a Code of Corporate Governance based on the 2015 OECD Guidelines on Corporate Governance of State-Owned Enterprises; and (iv) an accounting policy and procedures compliant with the Generally Accepted Accounting Principles. Also, the Palau Energy Administration has finalized regulations for setting cost recovery electricity tariffs, as well as for the development of renewable energy facilities by independent power producers.

In 2021, focus has shifted to implementing critical reforms in the water and wastewater sector. PPUC is similarly developing an annual revenue required model and revenue enhancement plan for water and wastewater, while establishing broader business analytics and performance disclosure frameworks to improve the utility's management and resource planning. The government is also looking to expand the Palau Energy Administration's mandate and convert it into an overall regulator of not only electricity but also water and wastewater

tariffs. More broadly, the government is pursuing other reforms aimed at elevating the performance of Palau's entire SOE sector, including developing a formal SOE performance monitoring policy along with a disclosure procedure for PPPs, including in energy and water supply, to allow for more informed management of contingent liability risks.

The timely completion of this ambitious reform agenda will facilitate simultaneous improvements in water supply service quality and revenue collections—through a gradual return to full cost recovery tariffs—toward breaking the current cycle of underperformance on both fronts. Financially sound water and wastewater operations, in turn, will help to further stabilize the overall performance of PPUC and reduce, if not eliminate, future subsidy needs for Palau's largest SOE. Along with broader reforms to the management of SOEs and potential PPPs, this can help free up vital fiscal space that will be critical for the eventual COVID-19 recovery phase, while also contributing to private sector development for broader-based economic growth moving forward.

CONCLUSION

Rationalizing government expenditures will be key to supporting post–COVID-19 pandemic recovery and ensuring longer-term fiscal sustainability in the North Pacific, especially after FY2023. Such expenditures include subsidies to SOEs, which have increased significantly in recent years. Managing these subsidies will require the implementation of reforms to improve SOEs' efficiency and commercialize their operations. Broadly, this could involve professionalizing management, including greater representation of women on SOE boards, and practicing timely and detailed record-keeping and financial reporting. For state-owned utilities and SOEs that provide other essential goods and services, ensuring cost recovery through well-crafted tariff regimes and CSOs, and improving revenue collection and infrastructure, will be important to maintain financial sustainability without sacrificing quality of output. Alternative mechanisms to provide services and social support can also help improve SOEs' efficiency and reduce subsidy requirements, thereby freeing up resources to support spending that is critical for post-pandemic recovery.

References

ADB. 2021. *Report and Recommendation of the President to the Board of Directors: Proposed Grant for Second Additional Financing to the Republic of the Marshall Islands for the Public Financial Management Project*. Manila.

ADB. 2021. *Report and Recommendation of the President to the Board of Directors: Proposed Grant for Second Additional Financing to the Republic of the Marshall Islands for the Public Financial Management Project*. Sector Assessment (Summary): Public Sector Management (accessible from the list of linked documents in Appendix 2). Manila.

Graduate School USA. 2021. *The Economic Impact of COVID-19 on the Marshall Islands with Policy Options for Sustained Recovery*. https://pitiviti.org/storage/dm/2021/06/rmi-updatingcovidimpact-2021-digital-remediated-20210625022732266.pdf.

International Monetary Fund. 2021. *Republic of the Marshall Islands: Staff Report for the Article IV Consultation*. Washington, DC.

Sustainable catch: securing economic benefits from fisheries in Nauru, Solomon Islands, and Vanuatu

Lead authors: Jaqueline Connell and Prince Cruz

As economies recover from the impacts of the coronavirus disease (COVID-19) pandemic, fisheries provide an important link for Nauru, Solomon Islands, and Vanuatu with the rest of the world. Although Nauru avoided economic contraction, disruption from COVID-19 led the economy of Solomon Islands to contract by 4.5% and Vanuatu's by 8.5% in 2020 (page 48). As countries seek to capture greater economic benefits from their fisheries resources, regional coordination, along with appropriate policies and public investments in infrastructure, will be critical to support a sustainable recovery.

The fisheries sector comprises two main areas: offshore and coastal fisheries. Offshore fisheries—harvested by large industrial fishing vessels—contribute to growth in foreign currency earnings through exports and license fees, and have linkages with domestic transport, storage, and food processing industries. Coastal fisheries, in contrast support subsistence and small-scale commercial fishing by local communities and play an important role in food security and nutrition.[1]

OFFSHORE FISHERIES

Despite their small land sizes, most Pacific island countries have large exclusive economic zones. Together, Pacific island countries supply about 50% of the world's tuna.[2] The fish catch is influenced by several factors, including fish migratory patterns, fishing access rights, and conditions that countries attach to access rights. In the longer term, climate change is also expected to affect the distribution and abundance of fish across the Pacific (*Future-proofing fisheries in the Federated States of Micronesia*, page 12).

Solomon Islands' exclusive economic zone at 1,589,477 square kilometers is about five times larger than Nauru's (308,480 square kilometers) and more than twice larger than Vanuatu's (663,251). Among ADB's Pacific developing member countries (DMCs), Solomon Islands has one of the highest average tuna catches, valued at about $426 million annually from 2013 to 2019; more than twice the $172 million for Nauru (Figure 13). For Vanuatu, average annual tuna catch was $117 million.

Fish exports, which come from domestically flagged (or registered) boats, can be volatile based on weather patterns and world demand. COVID-19 disrupted offshore fishing through shipping quarantine restrictions and the suspension of observers on purse seine vessels.[3] The value of Solomon Islands' fish exports fell by 12.0% in 2020.

Figure 12: Pacific Developing Member Countries Exclusive Economic Zones
(square kilometers)

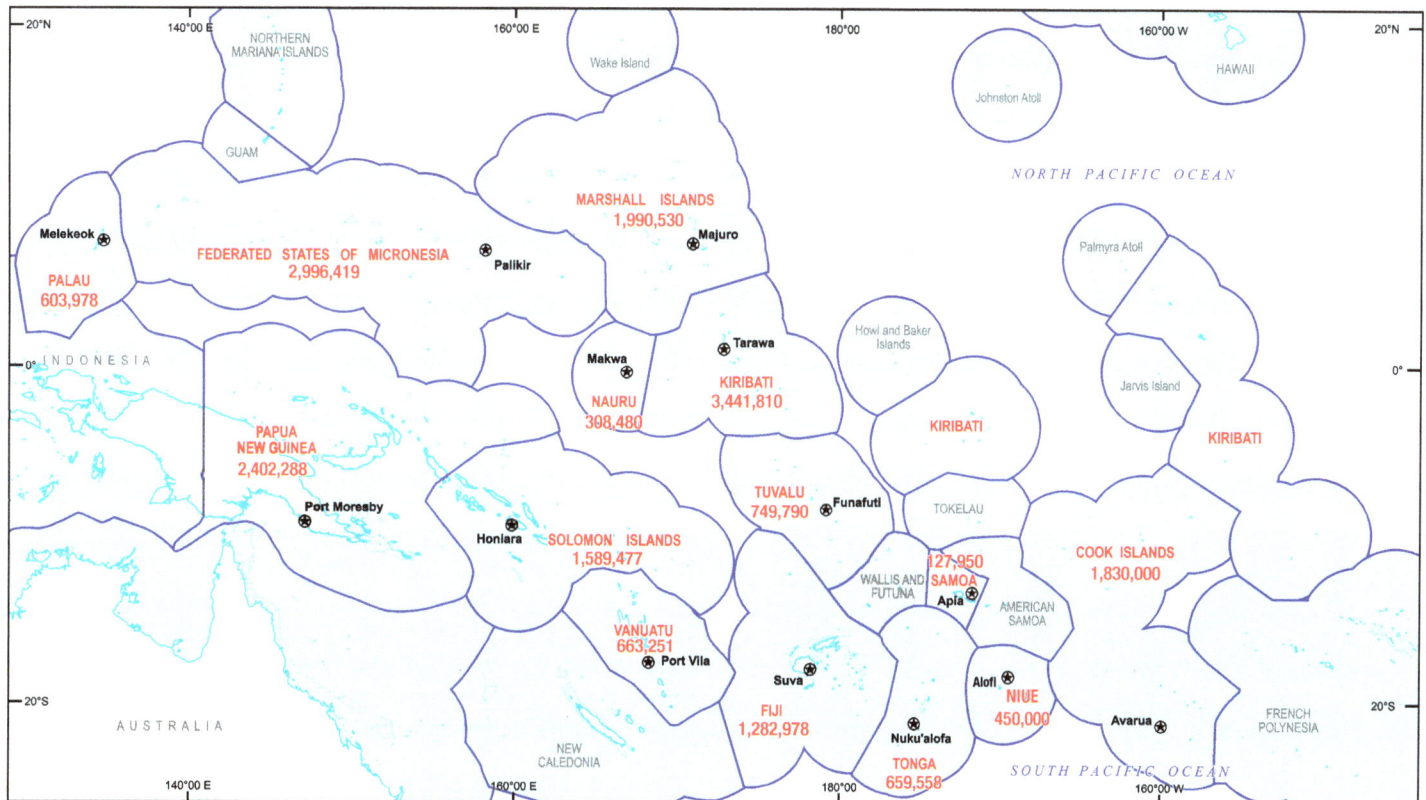

Sources: ADB. 2021. *Pacific Approach 2021-2025.* Manila; The Pacific Community. https://aquaculture.spc.int/index.php?option=com_content&view=article&id=13&Itemid=2.

After rising by 38.0% in the first half of 2021, Solomon Islands, fish exports are expected to exceed $50 million in 2021, up from $43.4 million in 2020. Although fish accounted for only 10.5% of Solomon Islands' exports, a distant second to logs and timber at 70%, the fishing industry is expected to be an important driver of growth for 2021 and 2022.

Figure 13: Average Annual Value of Tuna Catch, 2013–2019

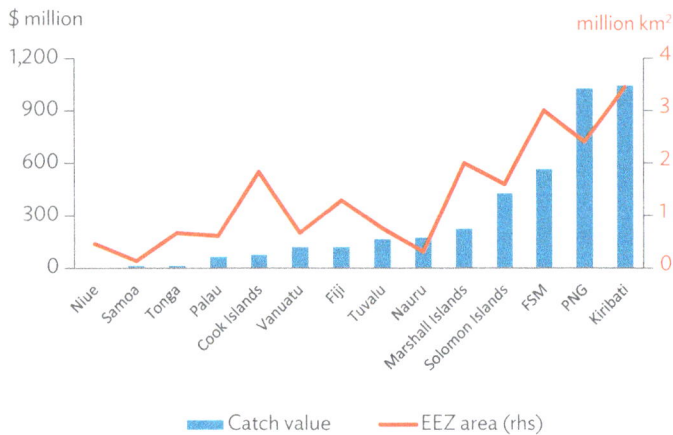

EEZ = exclusive economic zone, FSM = Federated States of Micronesia, km^2 = square kilometer, PNG = Papua New Guinea, rhs = right-hand scale.
Note: Catch value includes fish caught by the national fleet (domestically flagged and locally based foreign charters) and in national waters.
Source: Pacific Islands Forum Fisheries Agency. 2021. *Economic and Development Indicators and Statistics: Tuna Fisheries of the Western and Central Pacific Ocean 2020.* https://www.ffa.int/node/2596.

For Vanuatu, fish accounted for less than 3% of total exports from 2014 to 2019, and 3.6% in 2020. The increase in the value of fish exports from $0.3 million in 2019 to $1.7 million in 2020 illustrated the potential to grow Vanuatu's fishing sector from its relatively low base (Figure 14).

Figure 14: Vanuatu Fish Exports

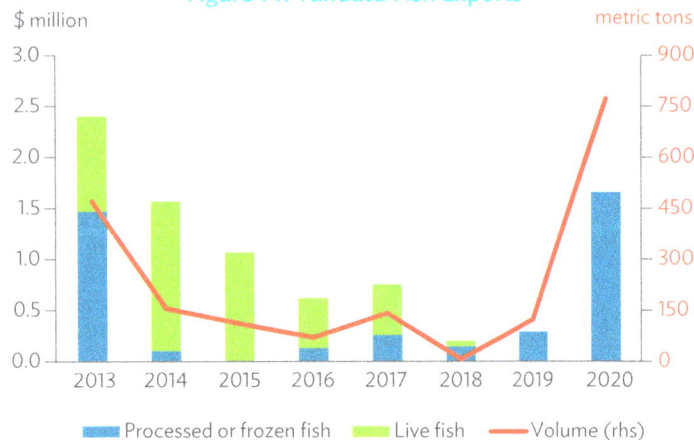

rhs = right-hand scale.
Note: Live fish include ornamental fish for aquariums.
Source: Vanuatu National Statistics Office.

An important way that countries benefit from their offshore fisheries is through selling licenses to foreign vessels for the right to fish in their territorial waters. Over the last decade, Nauru and Solomon Islands have seen large increases in fishing license fees, reflecting strong global market conditions and improved regional coordination under the Parties to the Nauru Agreement (PNA).[4] The PNA's focus has been the Vessel Day Scheme, which protects the sustainability of the regional fishery by capping the fishing days that member countries can sell based on scientists' advice about the status of tuna stocks.

Fishing license fees collected by Nauru and Solomon Islands increased to more than $40 million in 2019 from less than $20 million in 2010 (Figure 15). For Vanuatu, fishing license fees have remained at about $2 million annually.

Figure 15: Tuna License and Access Fee Revenue

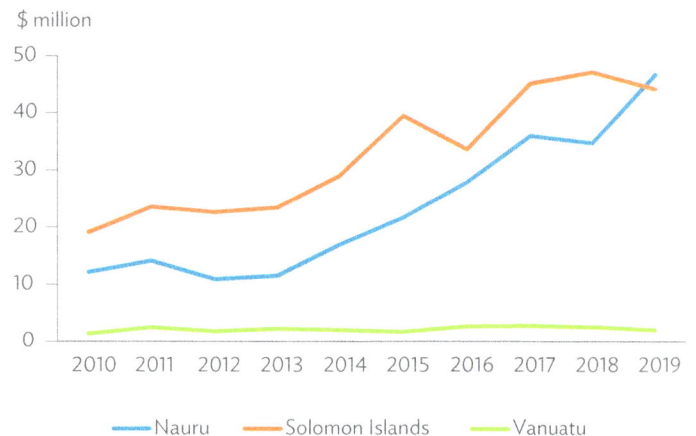

Source: Pacific Islands Forum Fisheries Agency. 2021. *Economic and Development Indicators and Statistics: Tuna Fisheries of the Western and Central Pacific Ocean 2020.* https://www.ffa.int/node/2596.

Through selling access rights to fish, Nauru has been able to capture large resource rents, even without having their own fishing fleet or processing plant. Fishing license fees received by Nauru were equivalent to 42% of gross domestic product (GDP) in fiscal year (FY) 2019 (ended June 2019) but declined to 30% of GDP in FY2021.[5] Key to maximizing development benefits from countries' offshore fisheries is ensuring that additional revenue from fishing licenses funds quality public expenditure. While increased government revenue has enabled higher spending in Nauru, the government has also saved about 10% of domestic revenue in the Nauru Intergenerational Trust Fund since 2017.

Over the years, efforts have been made to capture greater value from fisheries in several Pacific DMCs. This has included government and development-partner investments in fishing fleets and onshore tuna processing plants. The rationale was often that public investment was needed, in what is essentially a commercial operation, to support job creation and increase incomes. Unfortunately, most of the government-led tuna ventures created in the 1980s and 1990s proved unprofitable and are no longer operating.[6]

Despite their proximity to the natural fisheries resource, Pacific DMCs have faced challenges with developing competitive fish processing industries. Challenges include water scarcity for atoll countries, energy supply issues, and high labor costs relative to large competitors. Countries' small scale and remoteness also raise transport costs affecting imports of materials and exports of final products. Land ownership is another hurdle.

Nonetheless, there are some companies that are processing tuna in the Pacific. SolTuna, Solomon Islands' sole tuna-processing plant, has its own boats that deliver fish to their canning facility in Western Province where they are processed for local distribution and export. The company, which employs close to 2,000 people (or close to 1.0% of the country's workforce), is majority privately owned. There are also long-standing plans to develop a fish processing plant in Malaita, Solomon Islands' most populous island. Although Vanuatu has not had a fish canning operation since the Palekula Fishing Base closed in 1987, the government launched the joint venture, SINO-VAN Fisheries, in 2019 and fish production and export have since increased.[7] Nauru does not have a fish-processing plant.

While the risks and benefits of investing in commercial operations need to be carefully weighed, governments can play an important role in improving the enabling environment for private investment in fisheries and related industries. This includes ensuring that the policy, regulatory, and legislative framework is conducive to domestic and foreign investment.

Governments also have a critical role in delivering public infrastructure that supports business development. Poor transport networks are a brake on productivity, while the low level of electricity access outside the capitals of Solomon Islands and Vanuatu constrains local communities' ability to safely store their fish catch for consumption and small-scale commercial activities.[8] Along with energy access, improving wharves, ports, roads, and airports is critical, not only for fishing-related industries, but for broader private sector investment. The current construction of Nauru's first international seaport, for example, will improve connectivity and prospects for maritime trade.

Together with supporting the enabling environment for private sector development, governments have a role to ensure that offshore fisheries are sustainably managed so that future livelihoods, exports, and license fees are not compromised.

As fisheries are a migratory, shared resource, regional cooperation to manage them can provide benefits. Regional cooperation through the PNA helped create the world's largest sustainable tuna purse seine fishery. Many PNA conservation measures are world firsts, including controls on fish aggregating devices, high seas closures to fishing, and the 100% observer coverage on purse seine fishing vessels.[9] Solomon Islands has more than 100 certified observers, while Nauru has 40 to help ensure that foreign fishing vessels are operating within the regulations.[10]

COASTAL FISHERIES

Sustainably managing coastal fisheries is also important for improving food security, nutrition, and livelihoods. Although the overall economic contribution of offshore and coastal fisheries is small (at 6.1% in Solomon Islands, 2.3% in Nauru, and less than 0.5% in Vanuatu), a large portion of households engages in fishing.[11] While comparable data is limited, Solomon Islands is estimated to have one of the highest annual coastal harvests among Pacific DMCs. Adjusting for population, however, its coastal fish harvest is around the same level as Nauru's, while Vanuatu's coastal fish harvest is among the lowest (Figure 16).

Figure 16: Annual Coastal Fishing Harvest, 2014

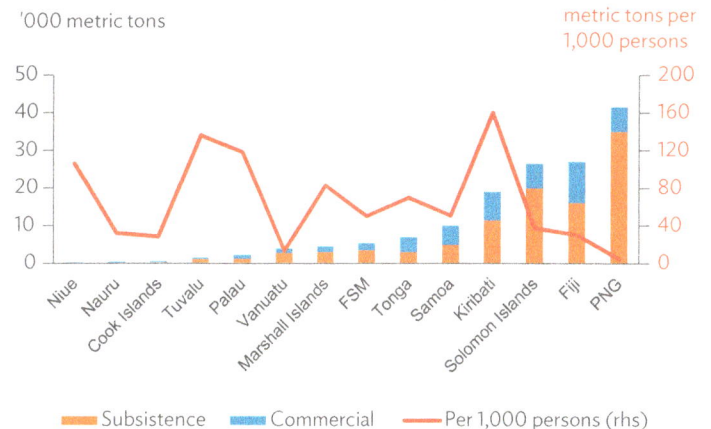

FSM = Federated States of Micronesia, PNG = Papua New Guinea, rhs = right-hand scale.
Note: Metric tons per 1,000 persons calculated using estimated population in 2020.
Sources: ADB estimates; Pacific Community. Pacific Data Hub. https://pacificdata.org/ (accessed 15 November 2021); and R. Gillett. 2016. *Fisheries in the economies of Pacific Island countries and territories*. Pacific Community, Forum Fisheries Agency, and Australian Aid. Noumea, New Caledonia.

Possibly reflecting the country's greater production of beef, the consumption of fish (and fish products) in Vanuatu is also the lowest among Pacific DMCs. There is also not much difference in fish consumption for coastal communities in Nauru and Vanuatu compared to the national level, unlike in Solomon Islands wherein coastal communities eat about four times more fish (Figure 17).

Subsistence fishing has dominated coastal fisheries. Less than 30% of the total coastal catch in Solomon Islands and Vanuatu is from commercial fishing each year. In Solomon Islands, less than 1% of households engage in aquaculture while only 2.6% of households engage in fishing mainly for sale. On the other hand, 10.9% of households engage in fishing for consumption (purely subsistence) while 21.2% engage in fishing for consumption and occasional sale, according to 2017 agricultural census. In Vanuatu, only 2.9% of survey respondents in 2016 said that they were engaged in fish or prawn farming while 49.0% said that they went fishing in the past 12 months, according to the 2016 census. To become net sellers of fish, subsistence fishers need reliable access to cold storage facilities and markets. Peddling fresh catch along the road or from house to house can lead to losses for fishers, discouraging higher output of fish and aquaculture.

Figure 17: Annual Consumption of Fish and Fish Products

kilogram per person

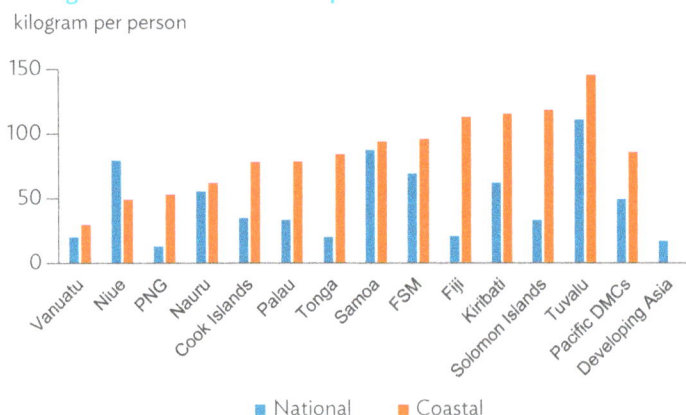

■ National   ■ Coastal

DMC = developing member country, FSM = Federated States of Micronesia, PNG = Papua New Guinea.
Note: Developing Asia includes Bangladesh, Bhutan, Cambodia, India, Indonesia, the Lao People's Democratic Republic, Mongolia, Myanmar, Pakistan, the People's Republic of China, the Philippines, Sri Lanka, Thailand, Timor-Leste, and Viet Nam.
Sources: Bell et al. 2008. Planning the use of fish for food security in the Pacific. *Marine Policy*. 33. pp. 64–76.; and S. Needham and S. J. Funge-Smith. 2014. *The consumption of fish and fish products in the Asia-Pacific region based on household surveys*. Bangkok: Food and Agriculture Organization of the United Nations Regional Office for Asia and the Pacific. RAP Publication 2015/12.

By increasing demand for coastal fish, COVID-19 raised concerns about the need to manage coastal fisheries sustainably. The Government of Solomon Islands encouraged people in the capital to return to their province as a precaution against COVID-19, while the loss of tourists in Vanuatu saw more people turn to coastal fisheries to support livelihoods and nutrition.[12] Even before COVID-19, minimal supervision or regulation of coastal fishing raised concerns on the sustainability of coastal fish stocks. Continued promotion and enforcement of sustainable fishing practices (such as identifying juvenile from mature catch) are necessary. Adopting policies and regulations in consultation with local communities can help maximize compliance while ensuring long-term sustainability.

POLICY DIRECTIONS

Recognizing the challenges and opportunities ahead, governments have put in place fishery policies. Recent developments include:

- In Nauru, the 2020 Coastal Fisheries and Aquaculture Act strengthens community engagement through locally managed marine areas and enables the Nauru Fisheries and Marine Resource Authority to impose regulations on coastal fishery activities to ensure that resources are sustainably managed. As Nauru explores options for deep-sea mining, the Nauru Ocean Resource Incorporated, which is responsible for deep-sea resource management, will need to ensure that potential environmental impacts on fisheries are minimized.[13] Although Nauru did not have a national tuna fishing fleet prior to 2018, it has since registered more than 20 purse seine vessels under its flag.

- In Solomon Islands, the Ministry of Fisheries and Marine Resources is guided by the National Fisheries Policy 2019–2029. After the government's policy redirection in 2020 prioritized the productive

and resources sectors, fisheries development focuses on strengthening the revenue contribution of commercial fisheries, providing opportunities for onshore processing, and enhancing small-scale fisheries contribution to food security and community livelihood. The government's 2021 development budget provided a 45.6% increase for fisheries compared with the 2020 revised budget (or a 300% increase compared with the 2019 actual budget) and included support for the Bina Harbour Tuna Processing Project.[14]

- In Vanuatu, after the passage of the revised Fisheries Act in 2014, the government prepared plans to develop the fisheries sector. These include the National Fisheries Sector Policy 2016–2031, the 2015 National Fishing Fleet Management Plan, and the Vanuatu National Roadmap for Coastal Fisheries 2019–2030. In 2020, the government approved the establishment of a Ministry of Fisheries, Oceans and Maritime Affairs to help expand and promote small-scale fishing opportunities, cannery processing, and other major fishery and ocean-related revenue-generating avenues.[15] The government aims to establish fisheries as one of the top 10 GDP sectors by 2030 and the 2021 Budget includes funding for boosting primary production (including fisheries) and strengthening agriculture value chains.

CONCLUSION

As countries seek to capture greater value from fisheries resources, governments have important roles to play. Although the risks and benefits of investing in commercial operations need to be carefully weighed, governments can take broader steps to increase the economic benefits of fisheries. First, careful fiscal management and expenditure prioritization can help to maximize the development impact of the additional government revenue from fishing licenses. Second, public investments that improve critical transport and energy infrastructure, together with policy reforms to create a stable, conducive business environment, could help facilitate higher levels of private investment in industries related to fisheries. Third, continuing to manage both onshore and offshore fisheries to ensure that they are used sustainably will help provide livelihoods, government revenue, and economic growth for present and future generations. When national interests can be aligned, regional cooperation to sustainably manage fisheries is likely to provide more benefits and allow countries to tackle larger challenges such as climate change.

Endnotes

1   A third category for coastal fishing is large-scale prawn farming which only exists in the Pacific in Papua New Guinea. Food and Agriculture Organization of the United Nations. 2018. *Fisheries of the Pacific Islands: Regional and National Information*. Apia.

2   The Pacific Community. 2019. *Healthy tuna stocks in the Pacific pave the way for strategic sustainable fisheries management*. https://www.spc.int/updates/news/2019/12/healthy-tuna-stocks-in-the-pacific-pave-the-way-for-strategic-sustainable.

3   Western and Central Pacific Fisheries Commission. *Coronavirus related measures*. https://www.wcpfc.int/covid19.

4   PNA members are the Federated States of Micronesia, Kiribati, the Marshall Islands, Nauru, Palau, Papua New Guinea, Solomon Islands, Tokelau, and Tuvalu. www.pnatuna.com.

5   Government of Nauru budget documents. Various years.

6   ADB. 2010. *Increasing Returns from Fisheries Do's and Don'ts for Policy Makers.* https://www.adb.org/publications/increasing-returns-fisheries-dos-and-donts-policy-makers.

7   International Monetary Fund. 2021. *2021 Article IV Consultation-Press Release; Staff Report; and Statement by the Executive Director for Vanuatu.* Washington, DC.

8   While electrification rate was 91% of households in urban areas in Vanuatu, it was only 54% for rural households in 2016. In Solomon Islands, only 16.2% of households outside Honiara had access to electricity, as against 45.4% in the capital in 2009.

9   In 2011, the PNA skipjack tuna (the most commonly canned tuna) caught without using fish aggregating devices was certified by the Marine Stewardship Council as sustainable. With effective controls on fish aggregating devices, no dolphins are caught in PNA waters and bycatch of other species is limited. www.pnatuna.com.

10 Government of Nauru. 2021. *Republic of Nauru 2021–22 Budget Paper No 2.* Yaren; Parties to the Nauru Agreement. 2021. *Certified Observers* (Last updated: 22 January 2021). https://www.pnatuna.com/index.php/certified-observers.

11 Contribution to GDP refer to 2017 for Solomon Islands, 2014 for Nauru, and 2018 for Vanuatu. The proportion of the population involved in fisheries varies significantly between different reports in the three countries. For Nauru, estimates of households engaged in fishing range from 26% in the 2012/2013 Household Income and Expenditure Survey to 51% in the 2011 Census. Food and Agriculture Organization of the United Nations. 2018. *Fisheries of the Pacific Islands: Regional and National Information.* Apia.

12 H. Eriksson et al. 2020. *Coastal fisheries in a pandemic: Solomon Islands and Vanuatu experiences.* https://devpolicy.org/coastal-fisheries-in-a-pandemic-solomon-island-and-vanuatu-experiences-20200729/?utm_source=rss&utm_medium=rss&utm_campaign=coastal-fisheries-in-a-pandemic-solomon-island-and-vanuatu-experiences-20200729.

13 Government of Nauru. 2021. *Republic of Nauru 2021-22 Budget Paper No 2.* Yaren.

14 Government of Solomon Islands. 2021. *Solomon Islands Government Year 2021 Approved Development Estimates.* Honiara.

15 Primarily, the Department of Fisheries will be removed from the Ministry of Agriculture, Livestock, Forestry, Fisheries and Bio-security. As the number of ministries in Vanuatu is limited by the Constitution, the Ministry of Justice will be abolished.

The long shadow of noncommunicable diseases in Niue, Samoa, and Tonga

Lead authors: James Webb and Isoa Wainiqolo

While timelines may differ, the eventual reopening of borders in the Pacific may mean that it is only a matter of time before all Pacific developing member countries will be forced to grapple with the risk of community spread of coronavirus disease (COVID-19). In Niue, Samoa, and Tonga, the prevalence of noncommunicable diseases (NCDs) and limited health system capacity to treat complex cases and isolate patients would exacerbate COVID-19 impacts. NCDs and obesity are prime risk factors for COVID-19 complications, leading to greater likelihood of severe illness, mortality, and ongoing symptoms ("long COVID-19"). It will require multi-sectoral efforts to mitigate the elevated risks to the population both now and into the future with possible variants of COVID-19 having potentially different transmissibility, severity, and immune response, as was seen with the Delta variant.

OBESITY AND NONCOMMUNICABLE DISEASES IN THE TIME OF COVID-19

While the implications of COVID-19 on populations with high prevalence of obesity and NCDs are yet to be fully understood, the World Health Organization (WHO) lists obesity as one of the highest NCD risk factors for severe COVID-19 infection.[1] The likelihood of requiring hospitalization is 113% higher, admission to intensive care is 74% higher, and the risk of death is about 48% higher, compared to the total population.[2]

Concerningly, obesity in patients aged 18 years and younger was associated with a threefold increase in risk of hospitalization and almost 1.5 times higher risk of severe illness.[3] Further, early research on "long COVID-19" suggests that more severe symptoms during the early stages of the virus lead to more persistent symptoms in the long term.[4] Aside from complicating the treatment of severe cases that may arise from breakthrough infections, obesity has also been shown to impair the development of immunological memory, possibly requiring more regular vaccine booster shots to maintain efficacy (endnote 2).

Vaccination remains the most immediate priority for protecting the populations of the Pacific from COVID-19. As of 22 November 2021, 75% of eligible adults in Niue have received their first dose of a vaccine and 72% are fully vaccinated; Samoa has issued the first dose to 92% of the eligible population and fully vaccinated 58%; and Tonga has issued the first dose to 95% of the eligible population and fully vaccinated 58%.[5] Niue will likely vaccinate children aged 12–15 years old in the coming months through the assistance of New Zealand, with Tonga and Samoa also considering vaccination campaigns for those under the age of 16 in December 2021.

However, vaccines will not be enough to fully protect populations from morbidity and possible deaths. The risks of waning efficacy in an obese population, a new variant possibly reducing vaccine efficacy, and breakthrough infections complicating the treatment of NCDs mean that underlying risks need to be urgently addressed. Concerningly, COVID-19 may have drawn the focus of the health system away from NCDs in the immediate-term, with regular screenings for NCDs likely to have fallen in most countries and public health messaging on NCD risk factors (unhealthy diet, smoking, obesity, and lack of exercise) likely to have been displaced by COVID-19 information.

NONCOMMUNICABLE DISEASES: THE HEALTH CRISIS THAT NEVER LEFT

Despite determined efforts to reduce the prevalence of obesity and NCDs, both remain entrenched public health problems. NCDs are the leading cause of morbidity in Niue, Samoa, and Tonga. COVID-19 has increased the urgency of addressing NCD risk factors, of which obesity is a particular concern.

Figure 18: Prevalence of Obesity Rates in the Pacific

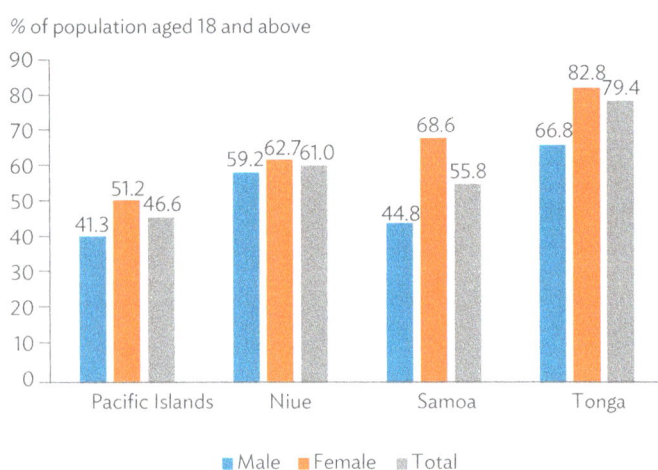

% of population aged 18 and above

Note: Data as of 2016.
Sources: WHO STEPS survey factsheets: 2013 (Niue and Samoa) and 2017 (Tonga); and WHO. 2018. *Noncommunicable Diseases Country Profiles* (Pacific). Geneva.

According to the WHO STEPwise Approach to Surveillance of Noncommunicable Diseases (STEPS) surveys, 79.4% of adults in Tonga, 61.0% of adults in Niue, and 55.8% of adults in Samoa were obese (Figure 18) with higher rates of obesity among women. These higher rates of obesity coincide with elevated risks of developing NCDs. In Tonga, 74.0% of the population aged 18–69 has been diagnosed with at least one NCD, and 98.7% of this demographic is at moderate to high risk of developing one: 27.6% had hypertension, 34.4% had elevated levels of blood glucose, and 48.8% had elevated levels of blood cholesterol.[6] For Samoa, almost 100.0% of the population is estimated to be at moderate to high risk of developing an NCD: 24.8% have diabetes and 24.5% have hypertension.[7] For Niue, about a quarter of adults had elevated blood pressure (23%) or blood glucose (26%) levels.[8] Heart disease, respiratory disease, cancers, and diabetes account for as much as 70% of all premature deaths in Niue and 80% of all premature deaths in Samoa and Tonga.[9]

With such a large proportion of the populations in Niue, Samoa, and Tonga having NCDs, the health systems of these countries were already under strain, facing difficult decisions regarding expenditure priorities. Health expenditures already account for a major share of government spending, but local health systems are unable to provide specialized treatment options with referrals for overseas treatment taking on a disproportionate share of overall health costs. In Samoa, for example, the cost for overseas referrals increased from ST0.3 million in 1991 to ST4.8 million in fiscal year (FY) 2015 (ended June 2015), equivalent to 10.0% of the national health budget but benefiting only 0.1% of the nation's population.[10] However, providing similar services in-country can also be a potentially costly exercise. The National Kidney Foundation of Samoa averaged ST56,312 per dialysis patient in FY2015, almost 5 times the average gross domestic product per capita and 100 times the average government health expenditure per person. The additional strain from managing COVID-19 complications in addition to underlying conditions may push health systems beyond their breaking point. Visiting medical programs, which almost all Pacific countries rely on for specialized medical services, have been disrupted because of border closures. This has presented challenges for basic NCD screening and continuity of case management. Further, overseas health referrals for critical or complicated treatment (especially for COVID-19 cases) may not be able to rely on previously established relationships. Intensive care units in-country are unlikely to be able to handle the caseload, with increased mortality a likely outcome if capacity gaps are not addressed. Reducing NCDs and obesity not only benefited the population prior to the pandemic, but in the longer term will reduce the strain that COVID-19 causes on national health systems.

NCDs also carry significant economic costs. The impacts of premature death from NCDs is estimated to reduce gross domestic product in Samoa by 8.5% in 2040 and by 12.3% in Tonga, primarily through a 12.4% and 18.5% loss in effective labor force.[11]

REDUCING NONCOMMUNICABLE DISEASES: REDUCING RISKS

This is a crucial time to strengthen Pacific leaders' commitment to implement the Pacific Islands Non-Communicable Disease Roadmap in line with the WHO recommendation on controlling NCDs,[12] and the NCD-related policy and legislation gaps identified in the Pacific Monitoring Alliance for NCD Action (MANA) Dashboard report. These recommendations include strengthening legislation and fiscal policies that address NCD risk factors such as tobacco, alcohol, unhealthy foods and drinks, and physical inactivity, as well as programs that promote primary and secondary prevention of NCDs. These actions, together with measures to reduce the spread of COVID-19 (such as vaccinations), will help shape, improve, and sustain physical, mental, and social wellbeing in the long term and contribute to achieving the healthy island vision.[13]

Given the current fiscal conditions from the COVID-19-induced economic downturn, tax measures on products known to increase risks of NCDs are a particularly low-cost solution which can also provide funding for additional health measures. In Niue, Samoa, and

Tonga, taxation has been particularly effective in reducing tobacco consumption. However, the popularity of tax measures is far from universal among populations and elected officials, and this may be an area where the sharing of cross-country experiences can significantly contribute to improved implementation and popular acceptance, noting the different realities between countries. For example, Tonga increased excise taxes on imported manufactured cigarettes by nearly 50% in July 2016. The resultant increase in cigarette prices contributed to reduced consumption, especially among lower-income groups. Impacts were diluted, however, by a shift to less expensive, locally made cigarettes (subject to lower taxes) and especially hand-rolled tobacco leaves (Tapaka Tonga, which are untaxed and contain more nicotine than manufactured cigarettes).[14] Similarly, increased excise tax on alcohol reduced consumption of alcoholic beverages, but demand shifted to other substitutes, such as kava. Evidence from the Cook Islands also suggests that signaling increases in excises in advance can induce stockpiling among suppliers if the government does not have adequate control measures, which can delay price increases and divert potential tax revenue that could have funded health interventions.[15]

Reducing the consumption of unhealthy food and drinks that are associated with NCDs is an important goal, but the effects of excise taxes on food are more mixed (endnote 11). Excise taxes on unhealthy food items like turkey tails, mutton flaps, and ice cream helped reduce consumption of these products in Tonga, though the tax had very limited effects on the consumption of chicken leg quarters. In addition, the tax on chicken leg quarters appeared to have regressive effects on poorer households. Despite the tax-induced price increase, chicken leg quarters remained the cheapest meat in the market, and less well-off households continue to buy it at similar levels, despite the higher price. The consumption tax-exempt status of selected healthy products (e.g., imported fruits) did not reduce retail prices or increase consumption, with benefits going to traders rather than households (endnote 14). In Tonga's case, availability, accessibility, and affordability of healthy food options remain major issues. A consistent approach using scientifically supported criteria across all food groups, including nutrient profiling that indicates unhealthy thresholds, is important for designing NCD tax policy. Some products deemed "unhealthy" may need to be reconsidered (e.g., chicken leg quarters or processed food in cans with high salt content) especially if nutritional benefits can be altered with preparation methods, if there are regressive effects of taxation, and if there are readily available substitutes.

Tax policy can be an important tool for reducing the risk factors associated with NCDs, but it should be complemented by other (non-tax) measures. For example, alongside tobacco taxation, Samoa also has extensive bans in place on promotion and sponsorship of tobacco, and graphic health warnings on smoking tobacco products. The WHO recommends that tax policies be important pillars for tobacco, alcohol, and sugar-sweetened beverages, but that these additional measures improve the effectiveness of mitigation efforts (endnote 11). Indeed, for unhealthy diets and increasing physical activity, the WHO recommends focusing on ingredient composition, product reformulation, reduced portion sizes, public awareness campaigns (for both diet and exercise), improved labelling, and increasing the availability of healthier food options. Both governments and development partners have made substantial efforts to improve the nutritional quality of available foods, but obesity rates continue to climb in all three countries. The WHO has identified obesity as one of the most serious health challenges for the region, particularly for the current generation of children.[16]

Alongside efforts to reduce the risk factors associated with NCDs, early screening forms another important pillar of NCD treatment efforts. Early intervention can also reduce lifelong symptoms, which would mitigate the need for costlier late-stage treatments and enable a better quality of life (endnote 11). For increased screening, the WHO-supported Package of Essential NCD (PEN) Interventions for Primary Health Care in Low Resource Settings identifies strategies for diagnosing and treating NCDs when adapted to each country's disease burden, risk factors, cost structures, and health system capacities. In Samoa, PEN interventions were introduced in Samoan villages in 2016 to improve early detection, improve referrals, and increase public awareness. The 2018 Care for Hypertension and Other Chronic Conditions in Samoa Survey found that communities engaging in the PEN Fa'a Samoa ("PEN the Samoan Way") program are more likely to be screened and receive treatment. The PEN Fa'a Samoa was driven by community groups, particularly women's committees, demonstrating the importance that community engagement and traditional structures can play in the promotion and delivery of critical health interventions.

CONCLUSION

COVID-19 has brought public health rapidly into focus around the world, but for Polynesia and the broader Pacific the management of NCDs must remain front and center. Vaccination against COVID-19 will provide a first line of defense against severe illness, but Niue, Samoa, and Tonga can act now to further reduce the potential impact of the virus on their national health by addressing NCDs and obesity through preventative and early stage interventions. Pharmaceutical and similar treatments will continue to play a vital role in treating NCDs, but limited resources mean that preventative measures and early screening will continue to play key roles in keeping total costs manageable and avoiding unnecessary complications in both COVID-19 and NCD case management. Social determinants of health also need to be addressed as part of broader lifestyle and cultural change, with support from multi-sectoral engagement, effective tax policy, and implementation of effective mitigation measures on unhealthy lifestyles.

Endnotes

1   World Health Organization (WHO). 2020. COVID-19 and NCD risk factors. https://www.who.int/docs/default-source/ncds/un-interagency-task-force-on-ncds/uniatf-policy-brief-ncds-and-covid-030920-poster.pdf.

2   Popkin et al. 2020. *Individuals with obesity and COVID-19: A global perspective on the epidemiology and biological relationships.* https://pubmed.ncbi.nlm.nih.gov/32845580/.

3   L. Kompaniyets et al. 2020. *Underlying medical conditions associated with severe COVID-19 illness among children*. JAMA Network Open. 4.6 (2021): e2111182-e2111182.

4   C.L. Hodgson et al. 2021. The impact of COVID-19 critical illness on new disability, functional outcomes and return to work at 6 months: a prospective cohort study. *Critical Care*. 25, 382 (2021). https://doi.org/10.1186/s13054-021-03794-0.

5   WHO. 2021. *Pacific Joint-Incident Management Team Epidemiological update for COVID-19*. Suva (as of 22 November 2021).

6   WHO. 2017. *Kingdom of Tonga NCD Risk Factors STEPS Report 2017*. Suva.

7   WHO and Samoa Ministry of Health. 2013. *STEPwise Surveillance of Risk Factors*. Apia.

8   WHO. 2018. *Noncommunicable Diseases Country Profiles*. https://www.who.int/publications/i/item/ncd-country-profiles-2018.

9   WHO Samoa NCDs Country Profile, 2018. Samoa has one of the highest death rates (81.8%) and illnesses rates from NCDs in the world (cardiovascular disease 34%, cancers 15%, chronic respiratory disease 5%, diabetes 9%, other NCDs 18%). Notably, Fiji is the only Pacific country with higher rates.

10 Government of Samoa. 2020. *Samoa's Second Voluntary National Review on the Implementation of the Sustainable Development Goals 2020*. Apia.

11 Hou, X., I. Anderson, E.-J. Burton-Mckenzie. 2016. *Pacific Possible Background Paper: Health & Non-Communicable Diseases*. Washington, DC: World Bank.

12 WHO. 2017. *Best buys and other recommended interventions for the prevention and control of NCDs*. https://www.who.int/ncds/management/WHO_Appendix_BestBuys.pdf.

13 WHO. 2015. Healthy Island Vision: Yanuca declaration on health in Pacific Islands Countries and Territories 2015. 11th Pacific Ministers for Health Meeting. https://iris.wpro.who.int/bitstream/handle/10665.1/12508/PHMM_declaration_2015_eng.pdf.

14 World Bank. 2019. *Using taxation to address noncommunicable diseases: lessons from Tonga*. https://openknowledge.worldbank.org/handle/10986/32063.

15 WHO. 2016. *Forestalling in the Cook Islands: lessons for tobacco taxation in the Pacific*. https://iris.wpro.who.int/handle/10665.1/13127.

16 WHO. 2020. *Regional Action Framework on Protecting Children from the Harmful Impact of Food Marketing in the Western Pacific*. https://www.who.int/publications/i/item/9789290619093.

Papua New Guinea: using special economic zones to boost trade and growth

Lead author: Abhimanyu Dadu, consultant, Papua New Guinea Resident Mission

Papua New Guinea (PNG) has indicated an intention to use special economic zone (SEZ) authorities as a way to diversify its economy away from its dependence on petrochemicals under a new regulatory framework. In December 2019, PNG passed the Special Economic Zones Authorities Act (the SEZA Act) that defines the regulatory framework and establishes an independent authority to regulate SEZs. Although not the first of its kind in the country, this legislation subsumes earlier definitions of economic zones, which were limited to free trade zones, to provide a broader definition for what would constitute SEZs in PNG and how their administration will be managed in the future.

This article examines (i) the evidence for and against SEZs, especially in Asia, as catalysts for economic growth and development; (ii) the existing environment for SEZs in PNG; and (iii) some recommendations on how PNG can improve the regulatory environment and use SEZs for broad economic growth, especially to support post-coronavirus disease (COVID-19) pandemic recovery.

SPECIAL ECONOMIC ZONES GLOBALLY AND THE PAPUA NEW GUINEA FRAMEWORK

Broadly, SEZs can be characterized by (i) a geographically delineated area, usually physically secured; (ii) having a single administration and management structure; (iii) fiscal and regulatory benefits for investors; and (iv) a separate customs area (duty-free benefits) with streamlined procedures. A combination of the purpose of the SEZ and the structure of the incentives generally categorizes zones into different kinds. In the case of PNG, SEZs are said to include free trade zones, export processing zones, freeports, enterprise zones, empowerment zones, urban free zones, single factory zones, marine industrial zones, science and technology parks, petrochemical zones, logistics parks, airport-based zones, and other variants. As these are listed in the SEZA Act, the legislation allows wide flexibility for the authority and the government to define the policy on SEZs.

EVIDENCE OF THE SUCCESS OF SPECIAL ECONOMIC ZONES

The evidence from ADB's Asian Economic Integration Report 2015 suggests that SEZs can catalyze, but are not a panacea for, trade and economic growth. The report estimated that in Europe and North America, countries with an SEZ had a higher export performance than those without, whereas in Africa and Latin America, countries with SEZs had lower exports on average (by 40% and 41%, respectively) than countries without an SEZ. Regional differences in performance are explained by a variety of reasons: barriers to trade, efficiency of governance and oversight, independence of SEZ governing authority, adequacy and appropriateness of labor supply, strategic location, and transparency standards.

In Asia, evidence suggested a positive relationship between the export performance of countries and the number of SEZs. A 10.0% increase in the number of SEZs in an Asian country was associated with a 1.1% increase in manufacturing exports. This was also determined by the choice of SEZ institutions. For instance, countries with an SEZ law and an independent SEZ authority showed a significant positive impact on export performance of 40% and 27%, respectively (Figure 19).

Figure 19: Impact of Special Economic Zones on Export Performance

% change in national exports

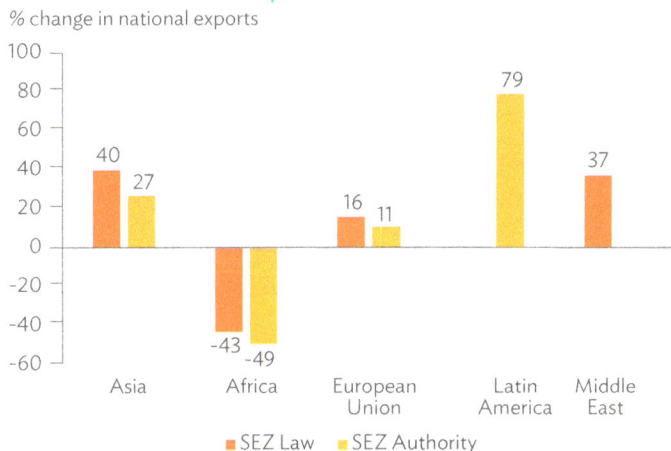

SEZ Law   SEZ Authority

SEZ = special economic zone.
Notes:
(i)   Effects estimated using dynamic gravity model with random-effects generalized last squares.
(ii)   For complete details of data and methodology, refer to ADB. 2015. *Asian Economic Integration Report 2015: How Can Special Economic Zones Catalyze Economic Development?* Manila.
(iii) Results are interpreted as the percentage difference in national exports as a result of the presence of an SEZ law/authority in a country compared with the absence of an SEZ law/authority.
(iv)   Results that were statistically insignificant have been zeroed.
Source: ADB calculations using data from UN Commodity Trade Database, CEPII, and national sources.

A similar estimation was conducted for the impact of SEZs on foreign direct investment (FDI) which showed that SEZs globally and in developing Asia also had a significant positive impact in attracting FDI (Figure 20). Existence of an SEZ is estimated to lead to 89.0% higher FDI for an economy globally and 82.4% higher FDI in developing Asia[1] compared to other Asian economies with no SEZs. This improvement in FDI performance is irrespective of the presence of an SEZ law or authority. In summary, the study found that, in Asia, chances of an improvement in export and foreign investment performance were higher with the presence of an SEZ in the economy and further improved under an SEZ law and/or an authority framework.

The socioeconomic impact of SEZs gets diffused through labor market outcomes by creating jobs and opportunities for women, increasing wages, improving health and security, and general labor conditions. The global evidence for such outcomes is limited to a few SEZs around the world. Improvements in export performance and foreign investment described above are often limited to the SEZ's strategic sector of focus, with many SEZs impacting only those sectors in which the country is already a substantial exporter. However, export diversification, which leads to diffusion of skills and technology, is limited to those countries that have been able to eliminate trade barriers in the wider economy.

Figure 20: Impact of Special Economic Zones on Foreign Investment

% change in FDI

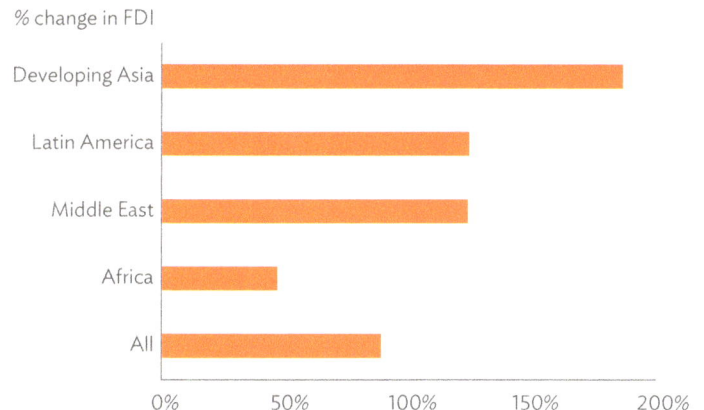

FDI = foreign direct investment, SEZ = special economic zone.
Notes:
(i)   Effects estimated using two-step generalized method of moments.
(ii)   For complete details of data and methodology, refer to ADB. 2015. *Asian Economic Integration Report 2015: How Can Special Economic Zones Catalyze Economic Development?* Manila.
(iii) Results are interpreted as the percentage difference in FDI as a result of the presence of an SEZ in a country compared with the absence of an SEZ.
(iv)   Results that were statistically insignificant have been zeroed.
Source: ADB calculations using data from UN Commodity Trade Database, CEPII, and national sources.

From these studies, a "key of success" for SEZs has emerged that can be summarized in a "stage-wise" structure of development. The first stage is creating fiscal, legal, and administrative structures targeted at export and foreign investment sectors. The second stage is the creation of forward and backward linkages with the economy to promote export diversification, and skill and technology diffusion. The third stage involves completing the development with national-level reforms fully integrating the zones in the national production structure. Very few economies have gone through all three stages (the People's Republic of China is the only emerging market example that comes close), which is also a reason why SEZ impacts are so mixed.

SPECIAL ECONOMIC ZONE POTENTIAL FOR PAPUA NEW GUINEA

PNG is a country in Asia and the Pacific with a $23.7 billion economy dominated by the export of oil and gas; mining products (gold, copper, nickel, and cobalt); and agricultural products (coffee, cocoa, palm oil, and logs). The three sectors together accounted for more than 95% of export earnings in 2019; 85% was from gold and liquefied natural gas. The investment climate suffers from structural challenges, including lack of infrastructure, labor skills, security issues, and land rights ambiguities. The country is also suffering from a lack of foreign exchange since the end of the last investment cycle in liquefied natural gas extraction.

The Prime Minister announced in 2020 that a 10-year tax holiday would be available for investments of more than $20 million.[2] The SEZA Act divides the entire country into economic zones, and concessions will be granted under delineated zones administered by the SEZ Authority and based on the economic advantages that the region offers. The government has already approved the development plans of a number of SEZs, before and after the passing of the SEZA Act (Table 2). While announcements have been made for SEZs in wide-ranging fields from tourism to blockchain technology, three SEZs are already in the first stage of development: the Sepik Plains SEZ in agriculture, the Pacific Marine Industrial Zone (PMIZ) in fisheries, and the Ihu SEZ in natural resources.

The PMIZ on the northern coast was the first SEZ to be advanced in PNG.[3] It was designed to establish 10 canneries for downstream processing by centralizing port and logistical hubs for PNG fisheries. PNG has a 2.4 million-square kilometer exclusive economic zone for fishing, consisting of substantial marine resources estimated at 18% of the world's tuna supply and 750,000 tons in annual tuna catch. A $95 million soft loan from the Exim Bank of China was approved in 2011 to support the development of the SEZ. However, the project has faced numerous challenges and delays since, with the loan facility expiring in 2016, having been drawn down by about only one third. In 2021, the government reaffirmed its faith in the fundamental advantage of the project in increasing value and creating jobs in the fisheries sector and announced a review of the project under the appraisal of the medium-term revenue strategy, although indicating that additional financing is needed, including for the development of port infrastructure.

The second major SEZ being advanced is the $31 million Sepik Plains agriculture SEZ, specifically designed to raise investments in a geographically isolated region. The plans include growing, harvesting, and processing of agriculture products along with housing, schools, police barracks, and aid posts for the workers and their families in a city-style framework. The government has already allocated funds from the national budget towards the development of social infrastructure and has signed its first joint venture agreement in 2018 for a $4.5 million commercial farming project and another for the development of the Sepik Oil Palm project. The project management is with the PNG Department of Commerce and Industry. The government has set up a state-owned enterprise, Kumul Agriculture Limited, to manage its stakes in joint ventures with the private sector with options for free equity granted to local governments and landholding groups.

Finally, the Ihu SEZ in the Kikori district of the Gulf province of PNG was the first SEZ to be approved after the passing of the SEZA Act and will be managed by the SEZ Authority. This zone is classified as an industrial downstream processing zone targeting exports in natural resources such as timber, fisheries, agriculture, minerals, oil, and gas. The central government provided $10 million from the 2021 budget and also signed on to $24 million in grant funding from the People's Republic of China for infrastructure development of the park. The zone seeks to encourage domestic investment and FDI by providing tax concessions and create local employment. Critically, the zone is not just about attracting new business. It also serves to help bring development to an area that is currently relatively isolated and lacks

Table 2: Potential Special Economic Zones in Papua New Guinea Listed in Schedule 1 to the Special Economic Zones Authorities Act

No.	Province	District	Type/Activity
1	East New Britain	All	Tourism
2	West New Britain	All	General
3	Autonomous Region of Bougainville	All	Agriculture
4	National Capital District	All	General
5	Central	All	General
6	Oro	All	Tourism
7	Milne Bay	All	Tourism
8	Western	All	Agriculture
9	Gulf	All	Industrial
10	Morobe	Finschhafen	Technology
11	Morobe	Markham	Agriculture park
12	Morobe	Huon Gulf	Industry
13	Madang	All	Marine and tourism
14	East Sepik	All	Agriculture
15	West Sepik	All	Agriculture
16	Western Highlands	All	Agriculture and general
17	Jiwaka	All	Agriculture and general
18	Hela	All	Petroleum and general
19	Southern Highlands	All	Petroleum and general
20	Eastern Highlands	All	Agriculture

Sources: Papua New Guinea Special Economic Zones Act, Schedule 1; and Deloitte. Tax Alert: Special Economic Zones Authorities Act 2019. https://www2.deloitte.com/content/dam/Deloitte/au/Documents/tax/deloitte-pg-tax-alert-april-2020-300420.pdf.

access to infrastructure and services. As such, it is appropriate to think about the project in wider terms than being just an SEZ.

EVALUATION OF SPECIAL ECONOMIC ZONE ARCHITECTURE IN PAPUA NEW GUINEA

PNG's planned foray into SEZs starts with incentivizing downstream processing and value addition in its abundant natural resources. The three SEZs identified all play to PNG's strengths. Unprocessed fisheries, agricultural produce, and minerals accounted for an estimated $4.6 billion in exports or 50.5% of PNG's total exports in 2020.[4] Most downstream processing is dominated by 1–2 foreign firms in each of these industries, with the agriculture and fisheries processing firms supplying primarily to the domestic market.

There is no visible link between SEZs and PNG's sustainable development strategy, although SEZs represent both a threat and an opportunity. PNG's forest and marine resources are the most abundant in the world, but are under threat of deforestation and overfishing because of lack of regulation. Poorly managed SEZs or lack of adequate regulatory requirement can accelerate these threats. However, the Green Growth Potential Assessment identifies opportunities to link the SEZ developments to off-grid renewable electrification, zoning regulations for forestry and commercial agriculture, and building administrative capacity.

The SEZA Act is a step towards consolidating the management and regulatory environment, but a number of challenges remain. The SEZs described above have been plagued with disputes between various government departments on the management of the project. They have come under judicial scrutiny for their land dealings, and fiscal incentives appear discretionary and uncertain.

If the government is serious about an SEZ regime, it would be imperative to link the policy to public finances. PNG's fiscal position has considerably weakened, especially after the pandemic, as public debt has jumped to the equivalent of 49.2% of gross domestic product in 2020 from 32.6% in 2016.[5] The inclusion of PMIZ under the revenue reform strategy is a step in the right direction, but it will also require links with a suitable expenditure strategy so as not to over-commit public resources towards SEZ infrastructure without the resources to finance it or knowing the returns on the projects.

The PMIZ will contribute towards building regional economic infrastructure. PNG is a signatory to Pacific Islands Forum of Fisheries Agency, Secretariat of the Pacific Community, and Western and Central Pacific Fisheries Commission. It coordinates with regional partners on the Vessel Day Scheme for tuna stock in the Pacific. The PMIZ will add to infrastructure capability to retain Pacific catch in the region and is an opportunity to promote economic growth and integration through these forums.

POLICY RECOMMENDATIONS AND SUMMARY

SEZs have the potential to boost economic growth, jobs, and trade in PNG. If executed and managed well, SEZs can attract foreign investment by functioning as zones that offer businesses access to raw materials, labor supply, supporting infrastructure and other facilities and services, a safe and secure environment in which to operate, and incentives.

However, if executed and managed poorly, SEZs have the potential to fail, becoming zones which have little more to offer than existing business locations, and which become a drag on the government's fiscal position.

Having strong policy settings and management in place to support the sound functioning of SEZs is therefore essential. This would entail measures such as having (i) a robust legal and regulatory framework with a high degree of transparency and accountability; (ii) prioritized land and resource use planning to balance long-term infrastructure development; (iii) calibrated fiscal incentives with national fiscal burden and use of sunset clause; (iv) a flexible labor market for unskilled and semiskilled workers; and (vi) an SEZ policy addressing basic infrastructure (water, power, telecommunications, and transport) provision and strategically integrated into the economy's overall development framework. Choosing appropriate locations is also necessary so that SEZs can attract both investment and workers to regions that need them the most.

Endnotes

[1] The impact is affected by the inclusion of effects for crisis years such as the Asian Oil Crisis (1998) and Global Financial Crisis (2008). This figure for developing Asia is with the inclusion of these effects, while for the rest of the world it is without the effects.

[2] However, Deloitte (2020) indicates a potential tax holiday of 15 years for companies that qualify.

[3] Oxford Business Group. 2016. *A high-priority marine industrial zone project breaks ground in Papua New Guinea.* https://oxfordbusinessgroup.com/analysis/zone-high-priority-marine-industrial-zone-project-breaks-ground.

[4] Quarterly Economic Bulletin statistics, Bank of Papua New Guinea, and staff calculations.

[5] Government of Papua New Guinea, Department of Treasury. National Budget documents.

References

Asian Development Bank (ADB). 2015. *Asian Economic Integration Report 2015: How Can Special Economic Zones Catalyze Economic Development?* Manila.

ADB. 2020. *Pacific Economic Monitor: COVID-19 Pandemic: Health, Economic, and Social Impacts in the Pacific.* Manila (July).

Deloitte. 2020. *Tax Alert: Special Economic Zones Authority Act 2019.* https://www2.deloitte.com/content/dam/Deloitte/au/Documents/tax/deloitte-pg-tax-alert-april-2020-300420.pdf.

Global Green Growth Institute. 2019. *Green Growth Potential Assessment - Papua New Guinea Country Report.* Seoul.

Government of Papua New Guinea. 2020. Special Economic Zones Authority Act 2019, Pub. L. No. 19 (2019). Port Moresby.

Zeng, D. Z. 2019. Special Economic Zones: Lessons from the Global Experience. *PEDL Synthesis Paper Series,* No. 1, 16 July.

POLICY BRIEFS

Modeling the Pacific's vaccine rollout

Every Pacific economy is, in some way, dependent—through tourism, remittances, services, or extractive industries—on the outside world. Border closures in response to the coronavirus disease (COVID-19) pandemic have devastated Pacific economies, and the Delta variant has spread to multiple Pacific island countries (PICs), causing immeasurable damage to lives and livelihoods. As the pandemic drags on, it is clear that in PICs, much like in developed nations, vaccination uptake is crucial to opening up to the outside world and enabling PICs to return to pre–COVID-19 ways of life.

In recognition of the region's dependency on imported vaccines, several development partners have pledged to send enough of the COVID-19 vaccine to fully cover the population of the Pacific (Figure 1). Australia committed to send 15 million doses of AstraZeneca to the region and Timor-Leste by the middle of 2022. In the North Pacific, the freely associated states of the Federated States of Micronesia, the Marshall Islands, and Palau have been included in the United States' schedule of COVID-19 vaccine distribution—also called Operation Warp Speed—managed by the United States Department of Health and Human Services. New Zealand committed to fully cover the needs of the Realm countries of Niue and the Cook Islands with Pfizer-BioNTech vaccines. The People's Republic of China pledged to support Pacific countries in their efforts to contain the spread of COVID-19 by rolling out the Chinese-made Sinopharm vaccine, mostly in Melanesia. Finally, all countries in the region are entitled to the COVID-19 Vaccine Access (COVAX) Facility, a global initiative to subsidize vaccines for lower-income countries led by the World Health Organization.

Figure 1: Vaccine Commitments to the Pacific
(% of total stock)

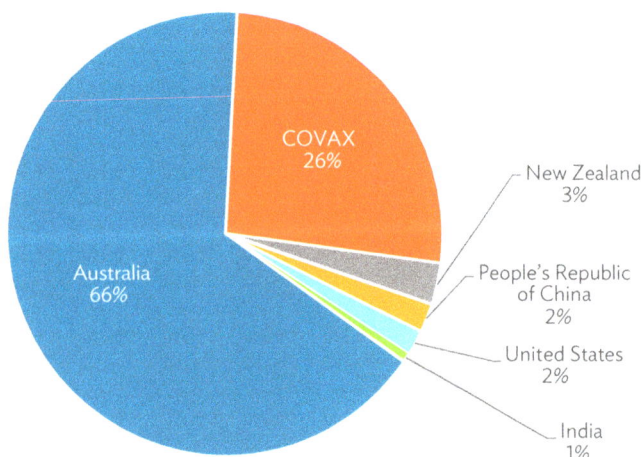

COVAX = COVID-19 Vaccine Access.
Sources: Think Global Health, government announcements, and author's calculations.

But vaccine supply is only the first of many hurdles. Rolling out a vaccine across one of the most remote, broad, and topographically diverse regions in the world is incredibly difficult from a logistical standpoint. The spread of misinformation throughout the region, especially in Melanesia, has compounded existing logistical, capacity, and governance constraints.

How well vaccines are distributed and administered will have significant health, social, and economic ramifications in the Pacific.

The Lowy Institute has developed a model to forecast the time it will take Pacific countries to vaccinate their populations. The model factors in two types of variables.

One set of variables is fixed and specific for each country. These variables are the size of the population, the urbanization rate, the number of health workers, and the number of vaccine doses that each health care professional can administer daily, using as a benchmark the current and projected vaccination rates in developing countries.

The other set of variables changes according to the evolution of the vaccine rollout. These variables are vaccine hesitancy, and the deployment of vaccinators across a country between urban and rural populations.

Vaccine hesitancy is the delay in acceptance or refusal of vaccines despite availability of vaccine services. In the model, it is inversely proportional to the vaccinated population, itself being context-specific, varying across time and country. As vaccination rates rise, so too do rates of vaccine hesitancy in the unvaccinated population as it becomes harder to find new unvaccinated people willing to receive vaccines. However, once a certain threshold of vaccination is reached, a demonstration effect occurs, reducing gradually the rate of vaccine hesitancy.

The distribution of health care workers across urban and rural settings is also assumed to change over time, according to the rate of vaccine rollout. Once vaccinations are completed in urban areas, vaccinators are expected to assist vaccination teams in rural settings.

Current vaccine rollout data were extracted from the Our World in Data series, which is maintained by researchers at the University of Oxford and the non-profit Global Change Data Lab.

As illustrated in Figure 2, the model shows that size is not everything, but when it comes to COVID-19 vaccinations, being small helps.

In August 2021, Niue was celebrated for reaching "herd immunity" in its fight against COVID-19 (Srinivasan 2021). In October 2021, Palau had the world's highest percentage of people vaccinated against COVID-19, with 99% of its eligible population vaccinated, while the Cook Islands had reached 96% of full vaccination (Reuters 2021). Others are fast approaching those targets, with the Federated States of Micronesia making vaccines compulsory for all adults (ABC News 2021a). Because of Nauru's relative size, the COVAX facility was able to guarantee supply for its entire adult population in a single shipment. As a result, almost all of Nauru's adult population received their first jab in a 4-week span (ABC News 2021b).

Figure 2: Projected Pacific Vaccine Rollout for Adults
(% of population aged over 18)

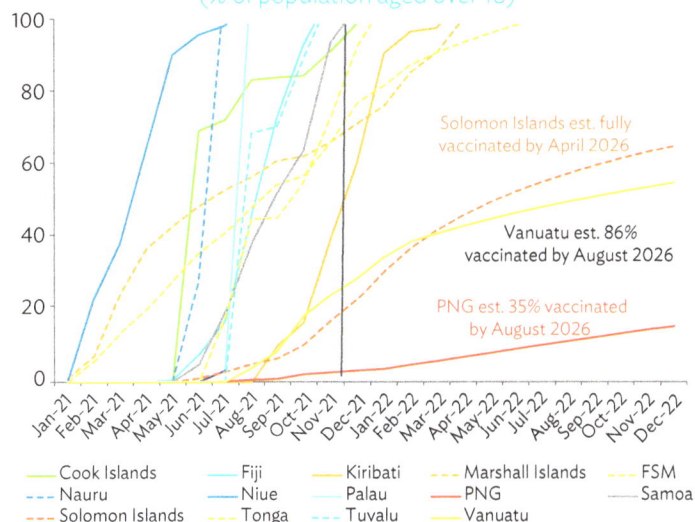

Solomon Islands est. fully vaccinated by April 2026

Vanuatu est. 86% vaccinated by August 2026

PNG est. 35% vaccinated by August 2026

Cook Islands	Fiji	Kiribati	Marshall Islands	FSM
Nauru	Niue	Palau	PNG	Samoa
Solomon Islands	Tonga	Tuvalu	Vanuatu	

est. = estimate, FSM = Federated States of Micronesia, PNG = Papua New Guinea.
Source: Author's calculations.

Other less-populous states such as Tonga and Samoa, thanks in large part to effective rollout campaigns and favorable geography with most populations concentrated on a select number of islands, look set to achieve similar milestones in late 2021 and early 2022, respectively.

Fiji is an outlier. As one of the most-developed nations in the Pacific, it was perhaps the best equipped nation in the region to manage a widespread Delta outbreak as well as a robust vaccination campaign, despite having the second largest population of the Pacific. Australia guaranteed supplies of vaccines and both Australia and New Zealand have provided additional support through the provision of medical assistance teams and other needed equipment and supplies. Thanks to the Government of Fiji's efforts, including measures such as a "no jabs, no jobs" policy for all public servants, the country has run one of the most effective vaccination campaigns in the world. After reaching a peak of over 1,400 new cases a day—the highest per capita rate of infections in the world at that time—Fiji is now recording a 7-day rolling average of 15 cases per day (Ritchie et al. 2021). The model estimates the country will fully vaccinate its adult population by the end of 2021, and its population above the age of 12 in the first quarter of 2022.

While those numbers are encouraging, the contrast with Melanesia could not be starker.

Vaccine skepticism is a key issue in Melanesia. Disinformation about the vaccine spread through social media has been identified by Papua New Guinea (PNG) Health Minister Jelta Wong as the "biggest challenge to efforts to curb the spread of the virus (Yahoo News 2021)." In Solomon Islands, early in the national vaccine rollout, Prime Minister Manasseh Sogavare expressed his disappointment in frontline civil servants who had not taken up the opportunity to receive their vaccinations (Government of Solomon Islands 2021). In addition to disinformation, this slow uptake has been driven by logistical challenges, capacity constraints, and a limited number of trained vaccinators. As of October 2021, only 9% of Solomon Islands' adult population had been fully vaccinated and, according to our model, the country will reach full coverage of its adult population by mid-2026.

Vanuatu's vaccine rollout has been similarly very slow, despite guaranteed supply from Australia, the People's Republic of China, and COVAX. As of October 2021, only 18% of the adult population had been fully vaccinated. The Government of Vanuatu aims to inoculate 60,000 of its population in 2021, just under 97,000 in 2022, and 161,000 in 2023 (McGarry 2021). Our model expects those targets to be reached with an average of 5–24 months delay, with 80% of the adult population being vaccinated by July 2025.

The situation in PNG is the most worrying.

A large rural population, difficult topography, limited logistical and health sector capacity, and low levels of staffing and resourcing create a challenging environment for PNG's vaccine rollout, but the major challenge has been widespread vaccine hesitancy and resistance across all levels of PNG society, fuelled by misinformation on social media platforms. Consequently, PNG had vaccinated only 2% of its adult population as of October 2021. If the situation remains unchanged, our model expects that only a third of the adult population will be vaccinated by April 2026.

While some countries are now focused on economic recovery and look forward to returning international visitors, PNG is struggling to cope with a humanitarian crisis.

When looking at the stark situation in Melanesia, the question of whether to vaccinate children can feel like a privilege. However, in the Pacific—a region that relies heavily on a few key external income sources—numerous countries look to vaccinate the population above 12 years old. In a region often qualified of "youth bulge," doing so would add a further 13% new cohort to the already slow vaccine rollout, resulting in larger delays for full vaccination, especially in Melanesia (Figure 3).

The challenge for Melanesia is not vaccine supply, but demand. How these countries address this challenge will define their economic and development trajectory for years to come. The model identifies two key variables that can improve vaccine uptake: increasing vaccine acceptance rates and increasing the number of vaccinators. Development partners, such as the Asian Development Bank, can help with both.

To increase acceptance rates, misinformation needs to be dealt with. Development partners should expand support to Pacific governments to boost their counter-misinformation campaigns. Vaccine hesitancy spans from the poor to the elite and the rural to the urban. Targeted, context-specific campaigns will be needed to identify who is trusted in local communities—religious leaders, sports icons, local politicians—and how they can be activated to campaign for the vaccine. For instance, a recent statement (Kokoda Historical 2021) by the PNG Council of Churches endorsed COVID-19 vaccinations, pushing back against increasing "vaccine apathy" caused by beliefs that the virus will not harm the pious (Ewart 2021).

Figure 3: Projected Pacific Vaccine Rollout with Pediatric Vaccination
(% of population aged over 12)

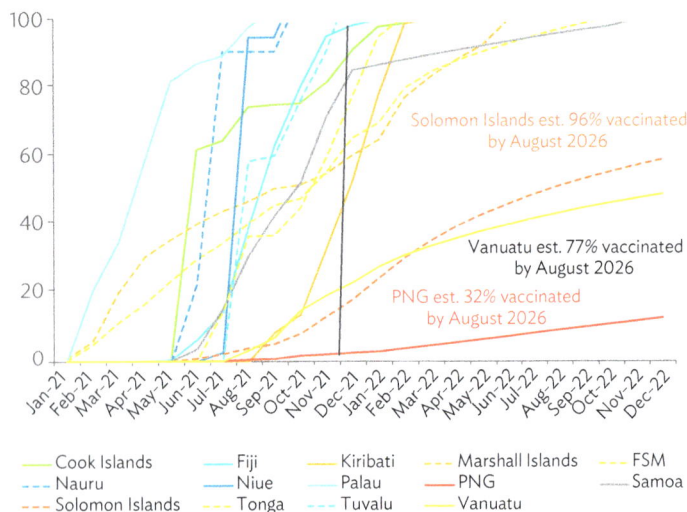

Solomon Islands est. 96% vaccinated by August 2026

Vanuatu est. 77% vaccinated by August 2026

PNG est. 32% vaccinated by August 2026

Cook Islands	Fiji	Kiribati
Marshall Islands	FSM	Nauru
Niue	Palau	PNG
Samoa	Solomon Islands	Tonga
Tuvalu	Vanuatu	

est. = estimate, FSM = Federated States of Micronesia, PNG = Papua New Guinea.
Source: Author's calculations.

Improving health sector capacity, and thereby increasing the number of vaccinators, is the other challenge. The pandemic has shone a light on many years of neglect within Melanesian health systems, and poor rates of vaccination for other diseases. Pre-existing issues, including a limited workforce supply, have been exacerbated and new threats, such as a lack of personal protective equipment and oxygen, have emerged. Development partners should engage in a suite of interventions, including partnering with overseas medical professionals, to bolster these countries' health systems not just for today but into the future.

With COVID-19-induced border closures creating large budget deficits, widespread unemployment, and other serious social implications, an unequal vaccine rollout will have lasting implications for the region's development. It is a race to get vaccines to all in need.

Lead author: Alexandre Dayant, Lowy Institute

References

ABC News. 2021. Federated States of Micronesia makes COVID-19 vaccine mandatory. https://www.abc.net.au/radio-australia/programs/pacificbeat/fsm-president-iv/13477078.

ABC News. 2021. Nauru gives first COVID vaccine shot to entire adult population in four-week campaign. 13 May. https://www.abc.net.au/news/2021-05-13/nauru-vaccination-coronavirus-covid-astrazeneca-covax/100137268.

Ewart, R. 2021. Vaccine apathy threatening to plunge Papua New Guinea into international isolation. Pacific Beat. ABC Radio Australia. 14 September. https://www.abc.net.au/radio-australia/programs/pacificbeat/png-vax-rates/13540742.

Government of Solomon Islands. 2021. Sogavare directs all frontliners to get vaccinated. 29 March. https://solomons.gov.sb/sogavare-directs-all-frontliners-to-get-vaccinated/.

Kokoda Historical. 2021. COVID vaccination in PNG. https://kokodahistorical.com.au/blog/covid-vaccination-in-png.

McGarry, D. 2021. Vanuatu coronavirus vaccine rollout to take until end of 2023. The Guardian. 26 February. https://www.theguardian.com/world/2021/feb/26/vanuatu-coronavirus-vaccine-rollout-to-take-until-end-of-2023.

Reuters. 2021. Tiny Pacific nation beats the world with 99% COVID vaccination, says Red Cross. 14 October. https://www.reuters.com/world/asia-pacific/tiny-pacific-nation-beats-world-with-99-covid-vaccination-says-red-cross-2021-10-14/.

Ritchie, H. et al. 2021. Coronavirus (COVID-19) Vaccinations. https://ourworldindata.org/covid-vaccinations.

Srinivasan, P. 2021. Pacific nations with high vaccination rates delay opening borders amid concerns around herd immunity. ABC News. 3 August. https://www.abc.net.au/news/2021-08-03/pacific-nations-covid-herd-immunity-borders-open-travel/100343634.

Yahoo News. 2021. Facebook virus lies 'biggest challenge' to PNG vaccine drive: minister. 1 April. https://au.news.yahoo.com/facebook-virus-lies-biggest-challenge-052248410.html.

Looking forward: toward the recovery of Pacific tourism after COVID-19

The coronavirus disease (COVID-19) has shaken the global tourism industry, previously considered one of the world's most resilient sectors. While many Pacific developing member countries (DMCs) have not experienced extensive transmission of the virus, they have nevertheless experienced widespread economic damage and the decimation of their tourism industries.

As global vaccination rates rise, the tourism industry is looking ahead to its recovery and considering how the sector can and should evolve post-pandemic. In the Pacific, increasing regional collaboration, improving the enabling environment for the private sector, evidence-based planning, and a focus on sustainability and future resilience could spur positive transformation as the industry looks to rebuild and grow.

IMPACT OF COVID-19 ON PACIFIC TOURISM

Tourism is vital to economic growth and employment in many of the DMCs. In 2019, it was the largest economic sector in the Cook Islands, Fiji, Niue, Palau, and Vanuatu, providing more than 20% of gross domestic product (GDP) and generating more than 35% of employment in all five countries. In the Cook Islands—the most tourism-dependent of the Pacific DMCs—the contribution of tourism to GDP was 66% in 2019 (Pacific Tourism Organisation [SPTO] 2020).

The pandemic has devastated many Pacific DMCs, particularly the most tourism-dependent. In 2019, the Pacific DMCs received a combined total of almost 1.8 million visitors by air, more than 320,000 by sea, and an estimated $2.7 billion in receipts (SPTO 2020). In 2020, these figures fell by more than 80% (SPTO 2021).

Pacific countries face growing unemployment and business losses. In Fiji, 37% of the country's labor force—131,000 people—had been made unemployed or had their working hours cut by August 2020 (Government of Australia, Department of Foreign Affairs and Trade 2020). In the tourism sector, the losses were even higher, with 80% of Fiji's tourism workers losing their jobs by October 2020 (Fiji Hotel and Tourism Association 2020). Similar losses occurred in the tourism-dependent economies of the Cook Islands, Niue, Palau, Samoa, and Vanuatu, and will have affected vulnerable populations—women, informal workers, and employees from rural communities—the most. For example, of the 26% of workers who had lost their jobs in Samoa by July 2020, 64% were women (International Labour Organization 2020).

RECOVERY CHALLENGES

The recovery of Pacific tourism is likely to be long and complicated. Tourist arrivals, flight frequency, and passenger loads into and within the Pacific DMCs will not reach pre–COVID-19 levels immediately or in the short term. Tourism Fiji, based on data from the United Nations World Tourism Organization (UNWTO), McKinsey, and tourism and airline bodies, has targeted of 13% of 2019 visitor arrivals for fiscal year 2022 (ends 31 July), 58% by fiscal year 2023, and a return to 2019 arrivals numbers by July 2024. A Pacific aviation industry study from October 2020 set the end of 2022 as the best-case scenario. The pessimistic case, which assumed border shutdowns continuing into 2021 and a lengthy wait for a vaccine, pushed this recovery into the second half of 2024 (Pacific Region Infrastructure Facility 2020).

While the concept of travel bubbles provides an opportunity for limited international air travel to resume safely, several bubbles already implemented in the region have come with significant challenges. A trans-Tasman bubble between Australia and New Zealand began in April 2021, a bubble between Palau and Taipei,China came into effect in April 2021, and a Cook Islands and New Zealand bubble opened in May 2021. However, all three bubbles have been suspended for significant periods of time following COVID-19 outbreaks in participating economies. In Palau, for example, the bubble was halted 7 weeks after opening because of a spike of COVID-19 cases in Taipei,China. During the time the bubble was operational, fewer than 300 tourists had arrived in Palau—about 2% of average pre-pandemic arrivals during April–May (ADB 2021). Despite the challenges, such bubbles have the potential to spur recovery; if Fiji entered a bilateral bubble with Australia, it was estimated that the drop in arrivals would be 44% compared with 84% under a "domestic tourism only" scenario (ADB 2020).

Resumption of tourism in DMCs will depend on vaccinations. As the virus is unlikely to be eliminated, a combination of widely available and effective vaccines, proficient testing, treatment and tracing, strong hygiene practices, and physical distancing measures will be critical to safely relaxing international travel restrictions (World Bank 2020). In Fiji, for example, the government's recovery strategy now rests largely on vaccination and slowing transmission of the virus, rather than elimination. The country reopened its borders to fully vaccinated international tourists from select countries on 1 December 2021. A successful resumption of international tourism, however, will also depend on decisions made by source market governments, such as travel advisory warnings and quarantine requirements.

Pacific DMCs themselves face a difficult decision once source market travel restrictions begin to lift. How much risk of importing a COVID-19 outbreak will they be ready to take on? That could at least partly be determined by their economic reliance on international tourism. Six—the Cook Islands, Fiji, Niue, Palau, Samoa, and Vanuatu—are considered severely dependent,[1] making an early return of international tourism critical.

Recovery rates will also depend on how much of a DMC's pre-pandemic tourism infrastructure has survived or can be quickly rebuilt. The full extent of bankruptcies and permanent closures is still not known, but Pacific DMCs rate poorly on indicators likely to reflect strong post-pandemic tourism resilience, such as having a well-equipped health system, good information and communications technology, high-quality tourist infrastructure, and a diversity of airlines and air connections. The unique combination of health, economic, and even psychological effects of this crisis is also likely to make the recovery uneven on both the demand and supply sides.

BUILDING RESILIENCE

The COVID-19 crisis also offers countries around the world, including the Pacific DMCs, the chance to build tourism back better. The shutdown highlighted some of the tourism economy's long-term structural weaknesses. These included fragmentation among tourism organizations and representative bodies, overdependence on international tourism, and inequitable dispersal of the industry's benefits. A build-back-better approach to recovery can begin to deal with these shortcomings and work on fully exploiting the acceleration of innovations the pandemic has also triggered, including widespread new uses for digital technologies. Success will require greater collaboration between governments, industry, and communities on tourism issues and policies to encourage lower carbon travel, ensure fairer distribution of tourism's benefits, and embrace innovation and digital technologies (Pacific Private Sector Development Initiative 2021).

The strategies that follow are aimed at helping Pacific DMCs to build their tourism industries back better, address long-term systemic challenges in the sector, and innovate. Four key areas have been identified for particular attention based on the analysis presented above. The strategies are not exhaustive, but rather offer an integrated, evidence-based initial approach to supporting tourism in the Pacific that is led by the private sector, good for local communities, and both resilient and sustainable.

A regional approach. In a time of crisis, cooperation can bring more benefit than competition. Pacific national tourism offices are faced with enormous expectations and limited budgets, particularly now with the COVID-19 pandemic disrupting global tourism. Collaboration among DMCs on some of the bigger challenges—such as crisis mitigation and resilience strategies, data analysis, and improving the enabling environment for tourism—would allow for best practice sharing, resource efficiency, and improved regional productivity. The Pacific Tourism Organisation (SPTO), the Pacific's primary intergovernmental organization for tourism, could help facilitate regional collaboration both in response to the pandemic and over the longer term.

Additionally, cooperation in destination marketing could build prosperous multi-country tourism. The Pacific could seek to promote multi-destination packages and capture tourists who stay longer and explore the region further. Destination differentiation could be part of the collaborative approach, to ensure each DMC is able to promote its unique and diverse cultural heritage as part of the regional "mix."[2] Conversely, if a competitive mindset among Pacific countries persists as borders reopen, it will raise the risk that a single destination will try to capture early bird travellers with discounted hotel and tour packages that others will have no choice but to match or better. Past experiences show that, once tourists have been offered discounted pricing, it can become what they expect and thus the new normal (World Bank 2020).

By taking a more regional approach, Pacific DMCs could also begin solving their individual transport connectivity problems. The Pacific's small and widely dispersed populations, spread across many islands, make it difficult for airlines to achieve sufficiently high levels of aircraft utilization and passenger loadings required to maintain profitability. Longer-term, greater regional cooperation or a more liberal multilateral approach in the aviation sector could enable more carriers to service major routes, reducing air transport costs and supporting sustainable tourism development as well as easing the pressure on local, state-owned airlines that may also be mandated to fulfill community service obligations alongside commercial operations. The fiscal resources that are freed up, as well as any additional revenues arising from more international arrivals, could be used to subsidize non-commercial but essential domestic routes and keep regional destinations connected (Pryke 2020).

Enabling sustainable, private sector-led tourism. Building more dynamic private sectors will help build bigger, better tourism industries and higher employment and incomes. COVID-19 has highlighted the importance of addressing outdated legal frameworks, cumbersome licensing and registration processes, and fluctuating and unpredictable regulatory requirements that are an unnecessary burden on growth and the contribution of private sectors. Streamlining for efficiency in the tourism sector also demands that manual and archaic processes be replaced by modern digital ones. Time wasted could be reduced and cost savings achieved, for example, by digitizing the licensing of tourism operators.

Poor access to finance was a serious problem for tourism small and medium-sized enterprises (SMEs) prior to COVID-19 and will be critical to the recovery. A DMC's otherwise liquid financial system will often limit these businesses' access to credit because of their perceived high risks or impose strict loan conditions that can cripple their development and growth. Banks may not accept the collateral available to tourism and other SMEs, and loan interest rates are notoriously high in some DMCs. But financing will have to come from somewhere if recovery efforts in the tourism sector are to gain traction. With their budgets already stretched by the effects of and responses to the pandemic, DMC governments could work with lenders to ensure more effective use of moveable assets as collateral and extend lines of credit to help SMEs stay afloat and give them the chance to rebuild.

Evidence-based planning. Robust indicators are essential for informing tourism policy and planning. However, in many instances, Pacific DMCs lack accurate, reliable data, resulting in a limited evidence base on which to plan future growth and against which to evaluate performance. Methodologies for assessing visitor spend and the contribution of tourism to both GDP and employment vary between countries and sometimes from year to year, which can lead to widely disparate figures. Employment data are rarely disaggregated, limiting a more detailed understanding of indicators such as gender. And the extent of economic leakage is not fully understood. Without these economic data, a full assessment of the benefits of tourism is not possible.

As borders begin to reopen, measuring the impact of tourism on supporting infrastructure, local culture, and the environment is vital to assessing the costs—as well as benefits—of the sector. Many DMCs list sustainability as a key goal. However, limited data on the impacts of tourism makes it impossible to assess the current position or plan a way forward with any certainty. Some DMC tourism plans propose ambitious visitor growth targets, but the sometimes-enormous levels of growth proposed are not evaluated against the likely economic, social, and environmental impacts of such growth. Reliable environmental data would also enable governments to set tourism targets beyond simply arrival figures, and target market segments based, for example, on their environmental impact.

Building sustainability and resilience. Economic and source market diversification, absent in many DMCs, is a key to greater crisis resilience. Pacific tourism industries are also often overly focused on a single source market, region, or tourist season. Diversifying in any one of these areas would add protection and make them less exposed to adverse change or shocks. Strategies to target new markets, preferably in different parts of the world, and build up arrivals in the periods between high and low seasons, for example through promotion of cultural or sporting events, could be included in DMC crisis management frameworks. So could action to improve local domestic infrastructure and connectivity to ease current DMC overdependence on international tourism alone.

Sustaining and maximizing revenue without increasing visitor numbers can build both resilience and environmental sustainability. Low-impact, high-spend tourism segments such as yacht visitors could be targeted ahead of traditional lower-spend but higher-impact tourists such as cruise passengers. Markets such as Papua New Guinea's that depend greatly on business visitors could develop more leisure activities for these travellers that would lengthen their stay and boost their spend. This strategy will be particularly valuable if tourist numbers take time to rebound.

Many Pacific DMCs still sit towards the bottom of development indicator tables, and limited data and analysis make it difficult to measure the impact of tourism on communities. Narrow indicators—such as arrival numbers—can essentially mask a more useful indicator, which is the value that the sector delivers in terms of its economic benefit, particularly to local communities. Reframing tourism aims and targets, while incorporating sustainability indicators, could not only lead to an improved understanding of tourism as a strategy for growth, but also help the Pacific DMCs build more sustainable, inclusive, and resilient tourism industries and derive greater value from the sector.

Lead author: Sara Currie, tourism expert, Pacific Private Sector Development Initiative

Endnotes

[1] Using indicators outlined by World Bank (2020). Severe dependence is a reliance on tourism for more than 20% of GDP.

[2] A destination differentiation strategy for four DMCs (Niue, Samoa, Vanuatu, and Solomon Islands) is currently being supported by the New Zealand Ministry of Foreign Affairs and Trade in partnership with SPTO.

References

ADB. 2020. Reviving Tourism amid the COVID-19 Pandemic. ADB Briefs: No. 150, Manila (September).

ADB. 2021. Pacific Economic Monitor. Manila (July).

Fiji Hotel and Tourism Association. 2020. Tourism Talanoa: Our Care Fiji Commitment. https://fhta.com.fj/tourism-talanoa-our- care-fiji-commitment/.

Government of Australia, Department of Foreign Affairs and Trade. 2020. Fiji COVID-19 Development Response Plan. Canberra.

International Labour Organization. 2020. ILO brief: Impact of COVID-19 on Employment and Business in the Pacific. Geneva.

Pacific Asia Travel Association. 2021. PATA: Growth Scenarios for Asia Pacific Fragile and Uneven to 2023. Press Release. https:// www.pata.org/press-release/pata-growth-scenarios-for-asia-pacific-fragile-and-uneven-to-2023.

Pacific Private Sector Development Initiative. 2021. Looking forward vol. 1: Evaluating the Challenges for Pacific Tourism after COVID-19. Sydney.

Pacific Region Infrastructure Facility. 2020. Post COVID-19 Pacific Short-term Aviation Strategy – A Scoping Study: Consultants' Final Report. Sydney.

Pacific Tourism Organisation (SPTO). 2020. 2019 Annual Review of Visitor Arrivals Report. Suva.

Pryke, J. 2020. Can Pacific airlines pull out of the dive? The Interpreter. 28 May.

SPTO. 2021. 2020 Annual Review of Visitor Arrivals Report. Suva.

United Nations World Tourism Organization (UNWTO). 2020a. January 2020 UNWTO World Tourism Barometer (English version). UNWTO World Tourism Barometer and Statistical Annex. 18 (1). Madrid.

UNWTO. 2020b. October 2020 UNWTO World Tourism Barometer (English version). UNWTO World Tourism Barometer and Statistical Annex. 18 (6). Madrid.

World Bank. 2020. Rebuilding Tourism Competitiveness: Tourism response, recovery and resilience to the COVID-19 crisis. Washington, DC.

World Travel & Tourism Council. 2021. Travel and Tourism Economic Impact 2021: Global Economic Impact and Trends. London.

Why does domestic resource mobilization matter for ADB developing members?

Small island developing economies, including many Pacific island economies, face distinctive challenges in public finance. These include volatility of domestic revenue because of reliance on narrow economic productive bases, such as natural resources or tourism, that are exposed to external fluctuations; high unit costs of providing public services to small and scattered populations; and significant fiscal and economic impact of severe climate events and disasters.[1] The coronavirus disease (COVID-19) pandemic has exacerbated these challenges. Unanticipated increases in public debt resulting from fiscal measures to mitigate the impact of COVID-19, and shrinking tax revenues during the pandemic, have worsened fiscal balances and created debt sustainability challenges in most Pacific developing member countries. Fiscal balances in 11 out of 12 Pacific economies worsened during 2019–2021, and the debt-to-gross domestic product (GDP) ratio of 8 out of 12 increased during the same period (Table 1). These issues require strong attention now because governments need to secure sufficient financial resources to contain the spread of COVID-19, procure safe and effective vaccines and health care, and get their economies back on a sustainable recovery track without losing market confidence.

Achieving Sustainable Development Goals (SDGs) is also important for the Pacific as it continuously faces the above-mentioned unique development challenges that have devastated local economies.

Efforts toward achieving the SDGs by 2030 will demand additional spending estimated to be equivalent to 6.5% of GDP.[2] External finance will be important in filling fiscal gaps, but domestic resource mobilization (DRM) will be crucial as SDG 17, which includes targets to strengthen DRM, is the foundation for achieving all of the other SDGs. Tax policy also offers governments the tools to achieve specific development goals under the SDGs. For example, governments can adopt a more progressive tax system to address the worsening income inequality because of COVID-19. Carbon tax or other environmental taxes can incentivize economic activities toward achieving green recovery, adaptation, and resilience.

Tax yields of many ADB developing member countries in the Pacific have been comparatively volatile in recent years (Figure 4). While most tax-to-GDP ratios in 2015 were above 15% except Papua New Guinea (PNG), those of the Marshall Islands and Vanuatu are only slightly above the benchmark.[3] These facts imply that there is some room for enhancing governments' ability to mobilize domestic revenue, enhance public services to their citizens, and achieve development goals. Additionally, for small states, while tax-to-GDP ratios were increasing, many of them rely on non-tax revenues (e.g., revenue from fishing licenses), which are often volatile sources of revenue that are not guaranteed in the future.[4]

Table 1: Fiscal Balances and Public Debt in the Pacific, 2019 versus 2021
(% of GDP)

	Fiscal Balance		Public Debt	
	2019	2021	2019	2021
Fiji	(4.4)	(12.7)	48.9	82.7
Kiribati	14.8	(11.4)	18.0	21.2
Marshall Islands	(1.7)	0.9	23.4	22.8
Micronesia, Federated States of	16.4	(3.2)	16.9	15.0
Nauru	20.5	16.2	62.0	57.6
Palau	0.4	(1.0)	32.5	40.6
Papua New Guinea	(4.4)	(5.4)	40.0	50.4
Samoa	2.7	(3.9)	47.5	49.4
Solomon Islands	(1.4)	(4.7)	8.3	22.3
Tonga	3.2	(1.7)	41.3	44.3
Tuvalu	(1.5)	(4.1)	16.2	13.9
Vanuatu	4.6	(5.8)	45.3	48.7

( ) = negative, GDP = gross domestic product.
Source: ADB. Asia Sovereign Debt Monitor database (accessed 21 June 2021).

Figure 4: Tax-to-Gross Domestic Product Ratios in the Pacific

% of GDP

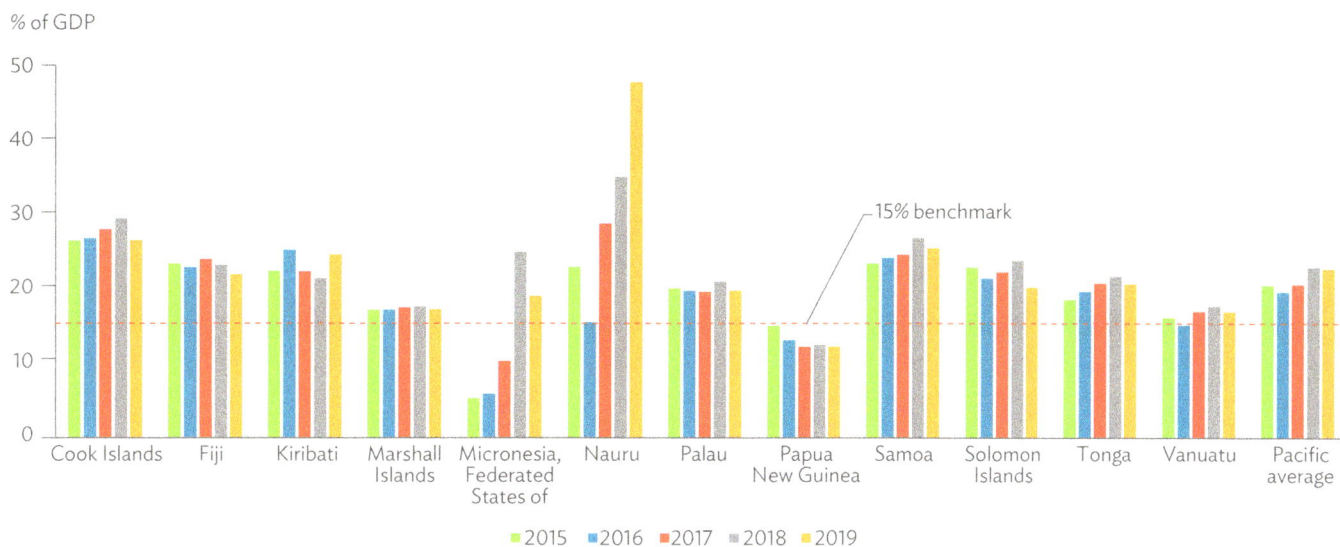

■ 2015   ■ 2016   ■ 2017   ■ 2018   ■ 2019

GDP = gross domestic product.
Sources: ADB. Key Indicators Database. https://kidb.adb.org/ (accessed 27 October 2021); Organisation for Economic Co-operation and Development. 2020. *Revenue Statistics 2020*. Paris; and World Bank. World Bank Open Data. https://data.worldbank.org/ (accessed 27 October 2021).

Thus, DRM will continue to be a major strategic priority in the aftermath of COVID-19 for developing countries, including the Pacific economies, to address debt sustainability and achieve the SDGs. In this regard, ADB considers DRM to be one of five strategic agendas to develop a prosperous, inclusive, resilient, and sustainable Asia and the Pacific.

Increasing domestic revenue requires consistent country-specific tax policy and administration efforts, coupled with continuous capacity development. Hence, revenue gains will take time to materialize, especially given limited capacity, large informal sectors, and narrow economic and tax bases in many Pacific economies. In this regard, preparation of medium-term revenue strategies (MTRSs) will perform a key role in supporting countries' efforts to enhance their DRM, meet their increasing spending needs, and achieve SDGs in the long term.

MEDIUM-TERM REVENUE STRATEGY AS A KEY TOOL FOR DOMESTIC RESOURCE MOBILIZATION

The MTRS is a multi-year and high-level plan for the tax system, embodying a government's strategy to mobilize resources for spending needs to achieve the SDGs and safeguard macroeconomic sustainability through, among others, domestic political commitment and secured external support for capacity development. The concept of the MTRS was developed in 2016 by the Platform for Collaboration on Tax, a partnership of the International Monetary Fund (IMF), Organisation for Economic Co-operation and Development (OECD), the United Nations, and the World Bank.

An MTRS is different from past or existing revenue strategies. It seeks to deal with deficiencies in these strategies by delineating differences between the current approach and an MTRS. The aim of an MTRS is to navigate various goals which cover equity, efficiency, and certainty in the tax system, tax morale, and other crosscutting

themes (endnote 4). The process for formulating a country-specific vision consistent with an MTRS should ensure that the following four independent components[5] are addressed (Figure 5):

(i)   a government's overall revenue goal over the next 4–6 years that is necessary for spending to finance its development goals,

(ii) a more comprehensive approach to tax system reform that covers tax policy, revenue administration, and the legal framework,

(iii) a sustained medium-term and whole-of-government commitment to reform, and

(iv) a coordinated engagement of external development partners in government-led tax reform.

Figure 5: Components of a Medium-Term Revenue Strategy

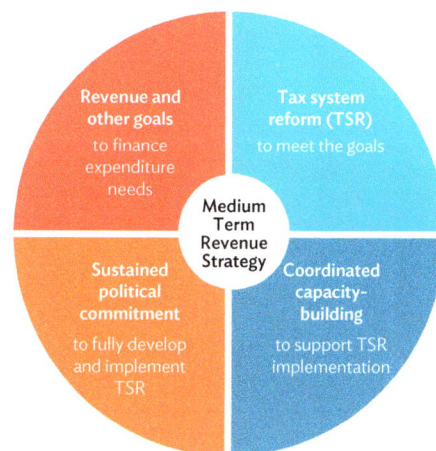

Source: Platform for Collaboration on Tax. Medium-Term Revenue Strategy (MTRS). https://www.tax-platform.org/medium-term-revenue-strategy.

Many countries in the region have been aiming to strengthen their revenue mobilization efforts through tax policy and administration reforms. Further, the COVID-19 crisis is adding urgency to the need for broad tax reform to conquer pressing challenges and improve tax systems. In this context, the MTRS approach will bring an opportunity for countries to develop and implement such strategies in a coordinated manner.[6]

MTRSs are now in various stages of development and implementation in 25 countries, including 11 countries in Asia and the Pacific (Box).[7] Of the latter 11 countries, PNG is the only country already implementing an MTRS.

Box: Medium-Term Revenue Strategy Workshop for Small States in Asia and the Pacific

In collaboration with the Platform for Collaboration on Tax, the Asian Development Bank organized a virtual workshop on 25–26 August 2021, which brought together more than 150 government officials, including finance ministers, from Pacific economies, Bhutan, Maldives, and Timor-Leste. The primary purpose of the workshop was to increase governments' understanding of the role that a medium-term revenue strategy (MTRS) can play in reforming their tax systems to meet revenue and other policy goals. Proactive discussion through exchange of expertise and experience took place during the event. Participants raised questions on how the MTRS relates to analytical tools like a gap analysis and the Tax Administration Diagnostic Assessment Tool, or how MTRS will be coordinated with other capacity-building programs already in place. This led to a better understanding among capacity-development partners on their role and how to coordinate their activities in the countries which plan to adopt, formulate, or implement MTRSs. The Asian Development Bank will continue to provide knowledge-sharing and capacity-building activities to build entry points for preparing MTRSs, in collaboration with the International Monetary Fund and other Platform for Collaboration on Tax partners.

Source: Platform for Collaboration on Tax. PCT-ADB MTRS Seminar: Medium-Term Revenue Strategies to Support Recovery and Development for Small States in Asia and the Pacific. https://www.tax-platform.org/news/event/pct-adb-mtrs-small-states-asia-pacific.

MEDIUM-TERM REVENUE STRATEGY IMPLEMENTATION EXPERIENCES IN PAPUA NEW GUINEA

Government revenues in PNG declined from 20.0% of GDP in 2011 to 13.2% in 2016.[8] The decline in revenue over this period was thought to be largely contributed by the fall in commodity prices, the adverse impact of disasters, and foreign exchange imbalances.

To address the fiscal stress, the Government of PNG sought support from the IMF and, on 28 November 2017, it became the first country in the world to embark on an MTRS. In May 2020, the government reconfirmed its commitment to the MTRS while updating some key milestones. Technical support formally commenced on 1 July 2018 and ongoing support will continue through the IMF's Pacific Financial Technical Assistance Center capacity development program and other development partners. The IMF support comprised advice on tax policy design, legal drafting, administration reform, and comprehensive missions. The Government of PNG also received support for MTRS implementation from other development partners including the Government of Australia, the World Bank Group, OECD, and the United States Treasury. While PNG is well supported by development partners, it is important to ensure that inputs are well coordinated to minimize the risk of duplication and conflicting advice.

To date, good progress has been made. For example, the Treasury set up a Revenue Policy Division to build fiscal planning capacity; the Treasury and the Internal Revenue Commission initiated the modernization and simplification of tax legislation; the Internal Revenue Commission established the Large Taxpayer Office and, together with the Customs Service, commenced core process improvements.[9] Notwithstanding the initial progress, there have been challenges along the way.

Program governance and interagency cooperation remain the biggest challenges to timely MTRS reform implementation in PNG. A disciplined approach to governance is critical for the success of any implementation plan and to ensure appropriate accountability of milestones and progress. Effective implementation and monitoring of any MTRS reform program also require detailed plans, such as an agency's annual plan, that can be clearly mapped onto the overall MTRS framework. Additionally, agencies would benefit from ensuring accuracy and quality of revenue data and having sound information management processes in place. Strong political support to enable timely passage of relevant tax legislation also plays an important role in facilitating implementation momentum.

Coupled with the MTRS process, a Tax Administration Diagnostic Assessment Tool (TADAT) was concluded for the Internal Revenue Commission in December 2019.[10] The TADAT aims to provide an objective assessment of the health of key components of the tax administration system, the extent of reform required, and the relative priorities for attention. This is another tool that a jurisdiction could employ in addition to an overarching strategy like the MTRS.

While there has been some progress with the MTRS implementation journey in PNG, there is still a long road ahead. As PNG's MTRS 2018–2022 implementation formally comes to an end, it is now focused on developing an MTRS 2022–2028. The successful development and implementation of this MTRS will go a long way to ensuring that PNG's future DRM needs are met. In an interview with authors of this article, PNG officials noted that other developing countries would have much to benefit in developing and implementing an MTRS.

NEXT STEPS WITH AN ASIA-PACIFIC TAX HUB

At a time when governments will seek approaches to increase tax revenues, they must build and maintain public trust by demonstrating that tax burdens are distributed fairly and equitably.

The Asia and Pacific region has emerged into economic prominence on the global stage. A recent ADB study found, for example, that this region accounts for about 48% of the digital economy globally. And the COVID-19 pandemic has accelerated the digitalization. The loss of potential revenues has been exacerbated by the absence of a multilateral consensus-based approach to tackle tax challenges arising from digitalization, which is estimated to cost $50 million–$80 billion per year,[11] while about $100 billion–$240 billion per year is lost globally in potential tax revenues because of base erosion and profit shifting. Therefore, international tax cooperation (ITC) is becoming increasingly significant for this region. Developing countries in Asia and the Pacific cannot afford to be indifferent but need to proactively engage in international tax initiatives and take full advantage of solutions that address aggressive tax planning and combat tax evasion.

ADB is committed to achieving a prosperous, inclusive, resilient, and sustainable Asia and the Pacific while sustaining efforts to eradicate extreme poverty. Of the seven operational priorities set out in ADB's Strategy 2030, operational priority 6 covers governance matters including DRM and ITC.[12] In this regard, the lack of a pan-regional tax community is a significant gap in DRM and ITC in Asia and the Pacific. There are some important tax communities in the region, but these lack a broad regional platform to engage in policy dialogue and represent a regional view on global policy discussions. To fill the gap, ADB officially launched an Asia Pacific Tax Hub in May 2021, which is envisaged to provide an open and inclusive platform for strategic policy dialogue, knowledge sharing and dissemination, and development coordination among ADB, its developing member countries, and development partners.

This Asia Pacific Tax Hub will support developing member countries by promoting three key building blocks in collaboration with key development partners, which cover formulating an MTRS together with the development of a road map for the digitalization of tax administrations and the assistance to achieve the effective participation in international tax initiatives. Under the Asia Pacific Tax Hub, ADB will proactively use financial instruments such as policy-based and project lending to promote DRM, adopt international tax standards, and strengthen technology investment by revenue agencies.

An effective collaborative framework is important to provide well-designed assistance and improve aid effectiveness. Effective coordination and collaboration with key development partners will maximize regional and international sources of knowledge, expertise, and finance on DRM and ITC. The synergy created in this approach will guarantee strong value-added and effective implementation of countries' tax system reforms.

Lead authors: Steven Fahey, senior tax specialist (consultant); Daisuke Miura, public management specialist (Taxation), Governance Thematic Group, Sustainable Development and Climate Change Department, ADB; and Go Nagata, public management specialist (Taxation), Governance Thematic Group, Sustainable Development and Climate Change Department, ADB.

Endnotes

1 Organisation for Economic Co-operation and Development (OECD). 2021. *Revenue Statistics in Asia and the Pacific 2021: Emerging Challenges for the Asia-Pacific Region in the COVID-19 Era.* https://www.oecd.org/tax/tax-policy/revenue-statistics-in-asia-and-the-pacific-5902c320-en.htm.

2 International Monetary Fund (IMF). 2021. Meeting the Sustainable Development Goals in Small Developing States with Climate Vulnerabilities: Cost and Financing. IMF working paper. Washington, DC.

3 Fifteen percent of tax revenue-to-GDP ratio is now widely regarded as the minimum required for sustainable development.

4 Platform for Collaboration on Tax (PCT). 2021. *PCT Regional Workshops on Medium-Term Revenue Strategies: Summary Report.* https://www.tax-platform.org/sites/pct/files/publications/PCT-Regional-MTRS-Workshops-Summary-Report.pdf.

5 PCT. 2020. *PCT Progress Report 2020.* http://tax-platform.org/sites/pct/files/publications/Platform-for-Collaboration-on-Tax-PCT-Progress-Report-2020.pdf.

6 World Bank. 2017. *Update on Activities of the Platform for Collaboration on Tax.* Washington, DC. (June).

7 PCT website. https://www.tax-platform.org/ (accessed 30 September 2021).

8 OECD. 2021. Revenue Statistics - Asia and the Pacific: Comparative tables. https://stats.oecd.org/index.aspx?DataSetCode=RS_ASI.

9 PCT. 2020. *Platform for the Collaboration on Tax 2020 Annual Report – MTRS Update.* https://www.tax-platform.org/sites/pct/files/publications/PCT%202020%20Annual%20Report%20-%20Appendix%20on%20Countries%27%20Medium%20Term%20Revenue%20Strategies%20Updates.pdf.

10 Tax Administration Diagnostic Assessment Tool (TADAT). 2021. TADAT, *Completed Assessments.* https://www.tadat.org/completedAssessments.

11 OECD. 2020. *Tax Challenges Arising from Digitalisation – Economic Impact Assessment Inclusive Framework on BEPS.* https://www.oecd.org/tax/beps/tax-challenges-arising-from-digitalisation-economic-impact-assessment-0e3cc2d4-en.htm.

12 ADB. 2018. *Strategy 2030: Achieving a Prosperous, Inclusive, Resilient, and Sustainable Asia and the Pacific.* https://www.adb.org/documents/strategy-2030-prosperous-inclusive-resilient-sustainable-asia-pacific.

Nonfuel Merchandise Exports from Australia
(A$; y-o-y % change, 3-month m.a.)

Fiji

Papua New Guinea

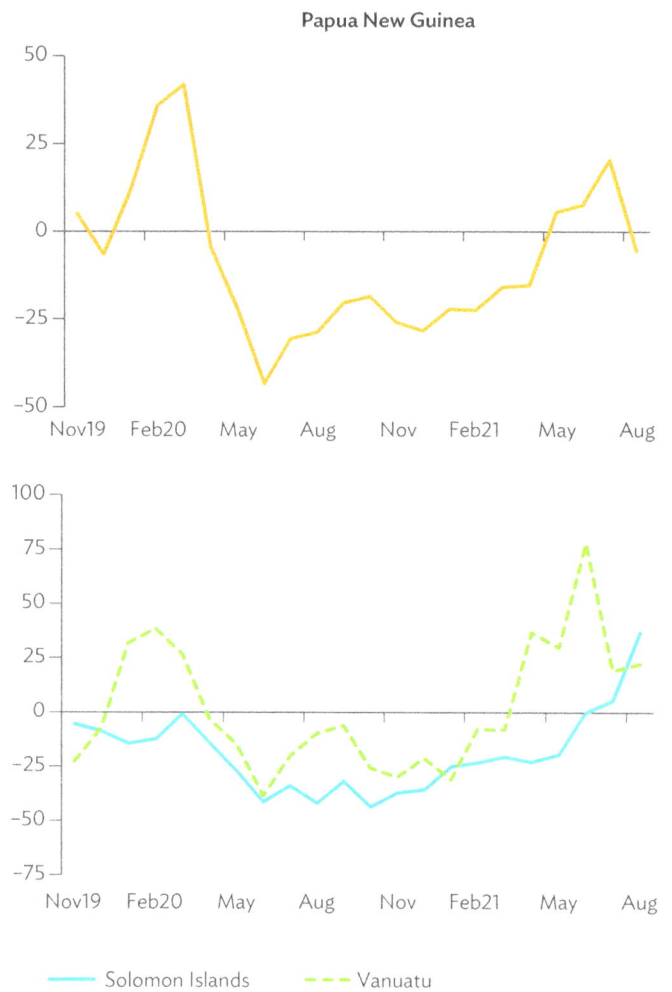

Kiribati ——   Nauru ······

Solomon Islands ——   Vanuatu ----

A$ = Australian dollar, m.a. = moving average, y-o-y = year-on-year.
Source: Australian Bureau of Statistics.

Nonfuel Merchandise Exports from New Zealand and the United States
(y-o-y % change, 3-month m.a.)

From New Zealand
(NZ$ million, fob)

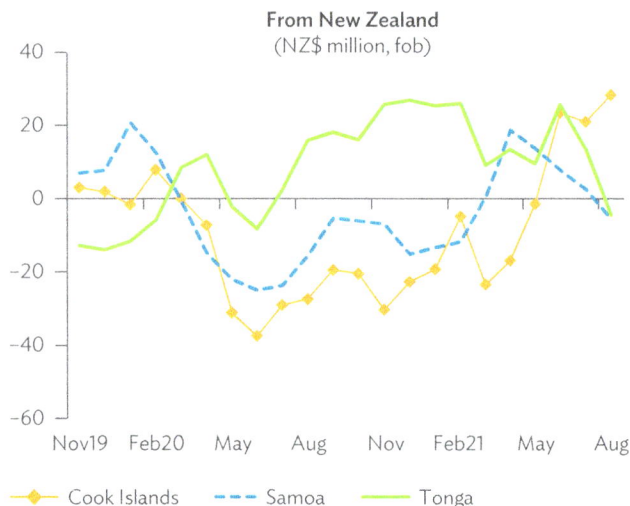

From the United States
($ million, fas)

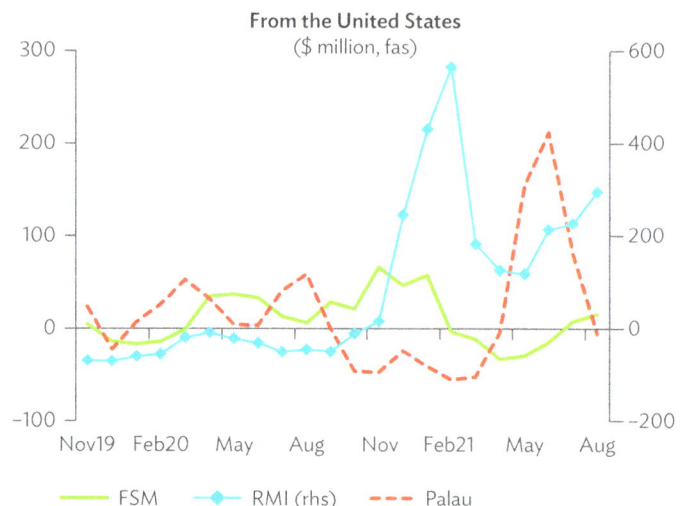

Cook Islands ——◆——   Samoa ----   Tonga ——

FSM ——   RMI (rhs) ——◆——   Palau ----

fas = free alongside, fob = free on board, FSM = Federated States of Micronesia, m.a. = moving average, NZ$ = New Zealand dollar, rhs = right-hand scale,
RMI = Republic of the Marshall Islands, y-o-y = year on year.
Sources: Statistics New Zealand and United States Census Bureau.

Diesel Exports from Singapore
(y-o-y % change, 3-month m.a.)

Fiji

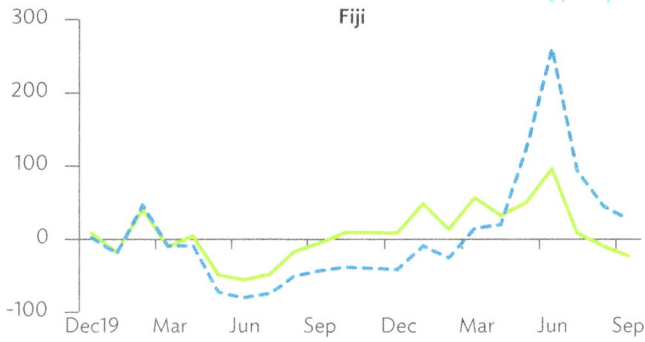

Papua New Guinea

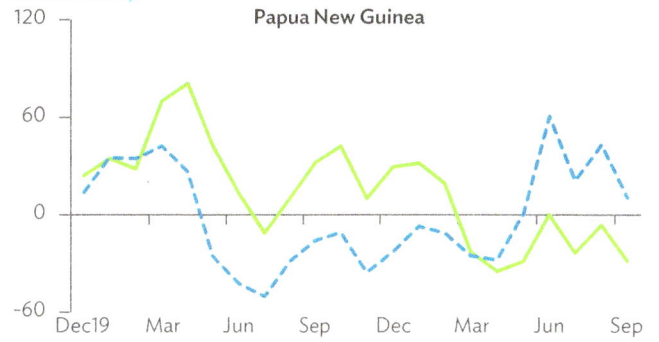

Samoa

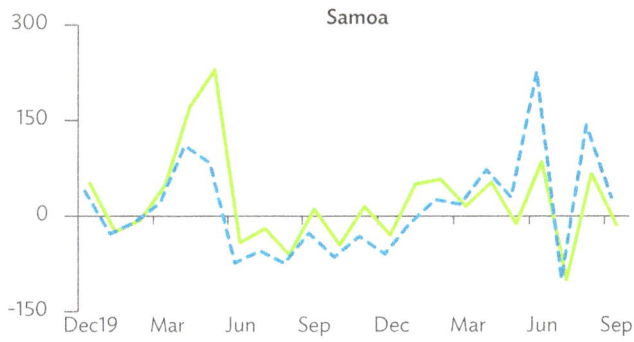

Solomon Islands

—— Volumes   - - - Values

m.a. = moving average, y-o-y = year on year.
Source: International Enterprise Singapore.

Gasoline Exports from Singapore
(y-o-y % change, 3-month m.a.)

Fiji

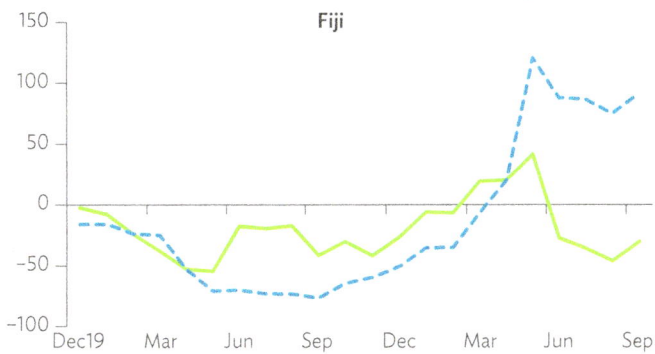

Papua New Guinea

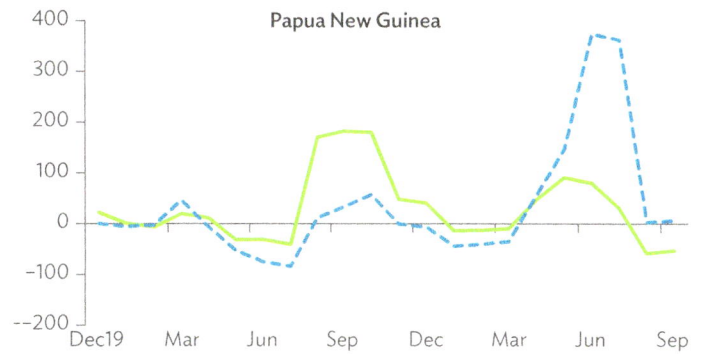

Samoa

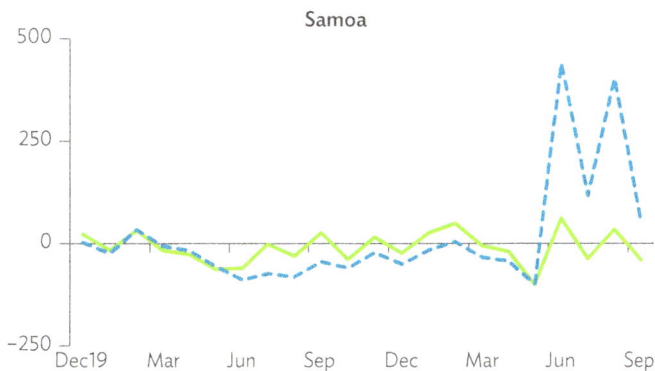

Solomon Islands

—— Volumes   - - - Values

m.a. = moving average, y-o-y = year on year.
Source: International Enterprise Singapore.

Departures from Australia to the Pacific
(monthly)

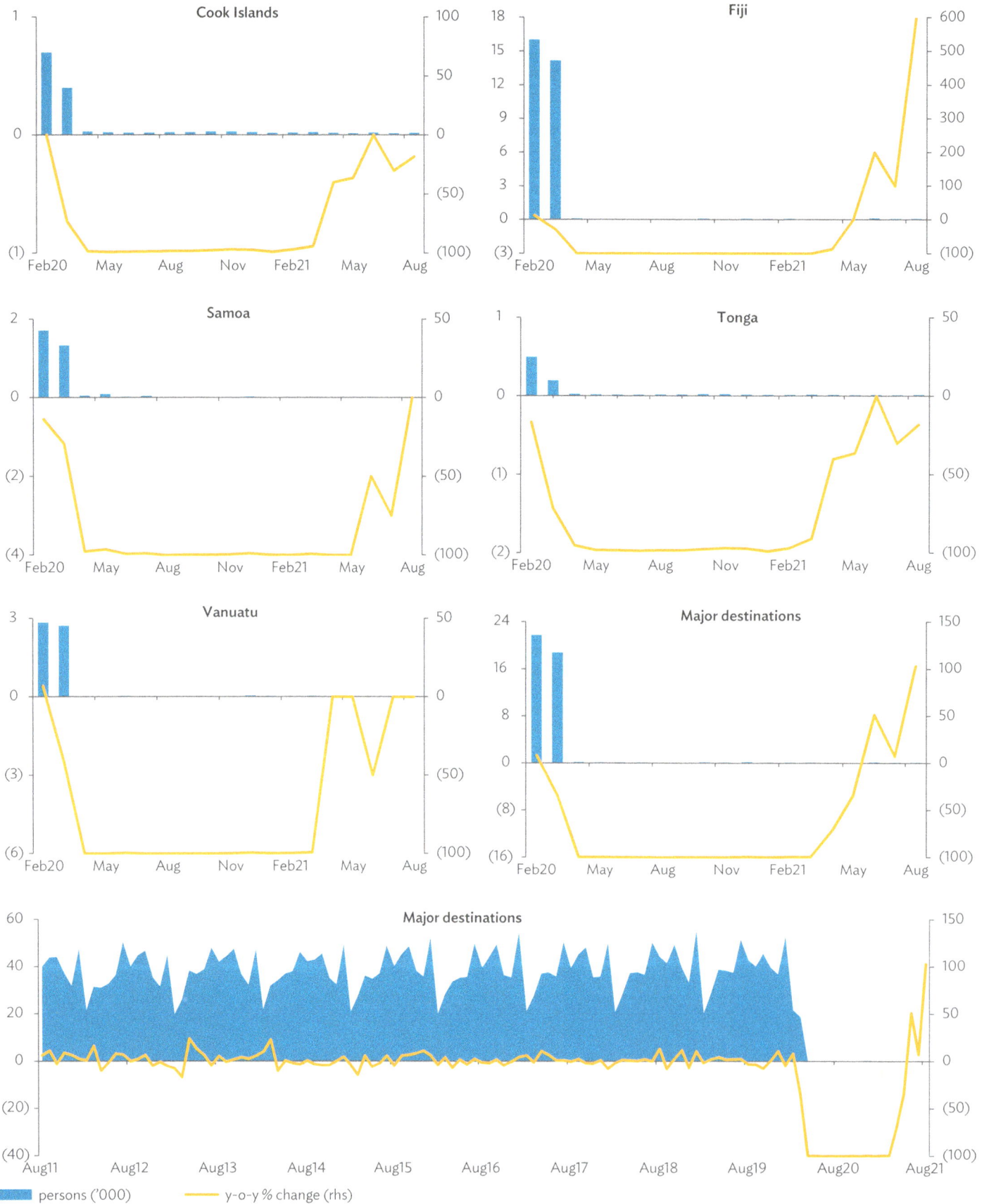

Cook Islands

Fiji

Samoa

Tonga

Vanuatu

Major destinations

Major destinations

persons ('000)   y-o-y % change (rhs)

rhs = right-hand scale, y-o-y = year on year.
Source: Australian Bureau of Statistics.